INTERPRETING

Interpreting
THE MIRACLES

REGINALD H. FULLER

SCM PRESS LTD

334 00681 3

First published 1963
by SCM Press Ltd
56 Bloomsbury Street London WC1
Tenth impression 1982

Printed in Great Britain by
Richard Clay (The Chaucer Press) Ltd,
Bungay, Suffolk

CONTENTS

Preface 7

1 THE BIBLICAL CONCEPTION OF MIRACLE 8
What is a Miracle? 8
Proofs or Signs? 11
Biblical Words for 'Miracles' 15

2 THE MIGHTY WORKS OF JESUS 18
Did Jesus Do Miracles? 18
Miracles outside the Gospels 20
The Gospels' Witness to Jesus as Miracle-Worker 24
Healings and Exorcisms 29
Nature Miracles 37
Jesus Interprets His Miracles 39
Faith and Miracles 42

3 INTERPRETING THE MIRACLES IN THE PRIMITIVE CHURCH 46
The Tradition in Q 47
The Marcan Material 48
Special Lucan Material 63
Conclusion 66

4 INTERPRETING THE MIRACLES IN THE SYNOPTIC GOSPELS 69
Five Groups of Miracles in Mark 69
The Messianic Secret in Mark 75
Ten Miracles in Matthew 77
The Meaning of Miracles to Luke 82

5 THE JOHANNINE SIGNS 88
The Book of Signs 88
The Evangelist's Interpretation 96

6 PREACHING THE MIRACLES TODAY 110
The Answer to John 114
The Marriage at Cana 117
The Dumb Demon 118
The Miraculous Draft of Fishes 120

Appendix 124

List of Gospel Miracles with Index 126

Index of Authors and Subjects 128

PREFACE

WHEN I received a request to write about the miracles of Jesus for the Religious Book Club of the SCM Press, I was already engaged to lecture on the same subject to a class of laity from the Diocese of Chicago in the Epiphany Term of 1961 at this seminary, and this book is based on that course of lectures.

My indebtedness to the New Testament scholars is apparent on every page, and it would be impossible to enumerate them all. I would mention, however, in particular the debt I owe to Dr Rudolf Bultmann and the younger disciples of the Bultmann school. It was my teacher at Cambridge, Sir Edwyn Hoskyns, who taught me to combine fearless criticism with an essential grasp of the evangelical message which is also Catholic orthodoxy. It is for the reader to judge whether I have been true to my teacher.

Biblical quotations in this book are for the most part taken from the American Revised Standard Version.

I

THE BIBLICAL CONCEPTION OF MIRACLE

What is a Miracle?

THE MAN in the street usually thinks of a miracle as something that happens contrary to nature. A more scholarly definition, approved by many modern theologians, is that of St Augustine: a miracle is an occurrence which is contrary to *what is known of nature*. This formula is attractive both for its scientific and theological humility. It admits that we don't know everything yet, that our scientific knowledge even in this twentieth century is still limited. But it is also prepared to surrender belief in a particular miracle, if it should turn out to be a natural occurrence after all. And on this definition the day may well come when we shall know so much about nature that there will be no place for a miracle after all.[1]

The Bible, however, knows nothing of nature as a closed system of law. Indeed the very word 'nature' is unbiblical. For the Bible the world is God's creation. This is thought of quite naively. God puts plants in the ground and makes springs of water for the wild beasts

[1] Recent philosophical discussion by Christians includes C. S. Lewis, *Miracles* (now in Fontana Books), and Professor Ian Ramsey's lecture *Miracles: An Exercise in Logical Mapwork* (Oxford, 1952). Professor Nowell-Smith states the philosophical case against miracles in his contribution to *New Essays in Philosophical Theology*, ed. A. Flew and A. MacIntyre (London, 1955).

to quench their thirst. He provides corn and wine to make men prosperous, and has appointed the sun and moon to mark the seasons and to provide a time-table for man and beast. Everything that happens in the realm of what we call nature is the handiwork of God himself. But in these operations his hand is invisible. No one has seen God doing these things at any time. His hand is seen more directly in unusual and terrifying occurrences like the earthquake and storm. These are acts of God's power, in which man has a more immediate experience of his hand.

But this is not all. Nature, whether usual or unusual, merely furnishes the stage for the major work of God. This takes place in the realm of history. Again, the Bible does not view history as the tranquil operation of God's 'providence'—another unbiblical word. Rather, history is the arena where God intervenes specifically from time to time, succouring men, pressing his demands upon them and judging them for their disobedience. It is these extraordinary interventions which, properly speaking, are the miracles of the Bible. They are not necessarily breaches of the laws of nature, or even of what cannot be known of nature. But they are sufficiently startling, unusual and unexpected to call attention to themselves. At the same time, however, they are not sufficiently unusual that they have to be explained as acts of God in the insurance company's sense of the word, as though we only call in God when all other explanations have failed. Rather, they are occurrences which faith recognizes as acts of God. Not that faith makes them acts of God. It merely recognizes them for what they are. But faith is always a free decision. It is never coerced by overwhelming proof.

In this sense of the word the two basic events in the Old Testament and the New are miracles. These are the Exodus and the Christ event, the foundation miracles of the people of God, of the old covenant and the new.

Each supreme biblical miracle is preceded by other, lesser miracles which call attention to the true significance of the supreme miracles and prepare for them. Before the Exodus come the plagues of Egypt and before the death and resurrection of Christ the healings, exorcisms (the casting out of demons) and the so-called nature miracles. The plagues of Egypt were preliminary judgements of Pharaoh, warning him of worse to come if he remained obdurate. The miracles of Jesus are preliminary rounds in the final conflict with the powers of evil, or the preliminary manifestations of the final revelation of the glory of God finally revealed in the cross.

In addition to these preliminary miracles ('signs' as they are called in Exodus and in the gospel of John) there are also what we may call 'accompanying miracles' occurring alongside of and as part of the great miracle itself. In the Exodus story the accompanying miracles are the dividing of the Red Sea, the pillar of fire by night and the cloud by day, the water from the rock, and the manna. In the New Testament the accompanying miracles are the conception of Jesus from a virgin, his baptism and transfiguration, the empty tomb and his appearances after the resurrection. They all accompany the Christ event to show that event to be the redemptive act of God himself.

The miracles associated with the great miracle do not end here, either in the Old Testament or in the New. In each case, after the supreme miracle has taken place, it is continued and extended in the on-going life of the people of God it brought into being. Israel's cultus, its worship, its sacrifices and its sacred feasts, above all the passover, are a 'remembrance' or memorial of the foundation miracle. This means more than the recollection of the great miracle as an event in the past, like the passion play at Oberammergau. Every devout Jew believed that in celebrating the passover he was transported across the centuries and enabled to participate in the supreme miracle itself. He was actually there, coming out of Egypt with his forefathers, crossing the Red Sea with them and entering into the promised land. The same is true in the New Testament. In the preaching of the word, in baptism and the Lord's Supper, the Christ event is not merely commemorated, but by the act it is brought out of the past and made effectively present so that the people of God can partake of its benefits. The word and sacraments are therefore miracles in the biblical sense. But they are not miracles in their own right. They are miracles only in so far as through them God makes present the supreme miracle of the Christ event.

Proofs or Signs?

Thus the biblical view of miracles runs counter to the accepted view of miracle as an occurrence contrary to the laws of nature or to what is known of nature. But it also runs counter to many other serious theological interpretations of the gospel miracles. Perhaps the one which had the longest innings was the view propounded (though it was much older) in William Paley's *Evidences of Christianity* (1794). For Paley, our Lord's miracles were *proof* of his divinity. This is wrong on two counts.

First, the divinity of our Lord is not just an abstract notion, a supernatural quality packaged within his human nature. Actually, the New Testament rarely uses the abstract term 'divinity' and never in respect of Jesus. It prefers to speak of God's presence and action, and of God present and acting in Jesus. Secondly, you cannot prove that an occurrence is an act of God: only faith can recognize it as such. Faith is not the mental acceptance of an abstract proposition, e.g. that Jesus is divine, but our total commitment to God's saving act. So you cannot prove his divinity by an occurrence which can be seen for what it is only by an act of faith. You cannot prove one article of faith by invoking another. Miracles are not proofs, but challenges to faith. They place us before an either/or: either they are acts of God, or, as Jesus' enemies held, they are black magic (Mark 3.22).

It was biblical criticism which undermined Archdeacon Paley's notion about the miracles. The earliest biblical critics, most of them Germans, were rationalists. They denied that Jesus did any miracles at all, for miracles could not happen. They were myths, the inventions of Christian credulity or products of misunderstanding. After the rationalists came the liberals.[1] They agreed with the rationalists about the nature miracles, but were prepared to accept Jesus' healings in so far as they could be explained psychologically and attributed to the influence of his personality on the sick. This meant, however, that they were no longer unique, and

[1] The classic treatments of Jesus in liberal Protestantism are those of the German, Adolf von Harnack, in *What is Christianity?* (London, 1901), and of the Cambridge classical don, T. R. Glover, in *The Jesus of History* (London, 1917).

that therefore they could no longer be regarded as proofs of Jesus' divinity. What then were they? Humanitarian examples! Here is a good summary of the liberal view:

> We are left then to suppose that our Lord was touched by the sight of suffering and that by the powers of his faith he was able to alleviate the pain of certain cripples, and that a few more incidents of kind actions must therefore be added to the history of humanitarianism, and that the Church, if it be the Church of Christ, must be persuaded to undertake more seriously the support of doctors in their work of healing.[1]

Far be it from us to decry the importance of humanitarianism. All we are concerned to insist on here is that it has little to do with the interpretation of the gospel miracles. Even Jesus' compassion, which is sometimes mentioned in the gospels as a motive for his miracles,[2] is not humanitarian compassion. As is indicated by the broader context in which the word is sometimes used,[3] and by Matthew's normal preference for 'mercy'[4] in the context of Jesus' healings, the compassion or mercy of which the evangelists speak is the compassion and mercy of God. It is Messianic, not humanitarian compassion. Nor is compassion simply the *motive*: the miracles are the direct act of God's compassion. That is

[1] E. C. Hoskyns, *Cambridge Sermons* (London, 1938), p. 58. Hoskyns does not, of course, accept this view.

[2] Mark 1.41 (some MSS. read 'was angry'); 6.34; 8.2; 9.22 (Matt. 17.15 substitutes 'have mercy'); Matt. 20.34 (inserted into a Markan passage).

[3] Matt. 9.36; Luke 10.33; 15.20.

[4] In addition to Matt. 17.15 (note 2 above) see 9.27; 15.22; 20.30 f.; and the citation of Hos. 6.6 in connection wth miracles at 9.13; cf. 12.7.

why compassion is only *one* of the words—and a comparatively rare one at that—which is used to describe the miracles. Other terms, as we shall see, are more characteristic, like 'mighty work', 'sign' and 'work'.

Since the decline of theological liberalism, the humanitarian interpretation has been replaced by a more biblical approach. While agreeing on the whole with the liberals' sceptical attitude to the nature miracles, the biblical theologians interpret the healings and exorcisms as signs, rather than proofs, of Jesus' Messiahship. This, broadly speaking, is the view of E. C. Hoskyns, Vincent Taylor, T. W. Manson, W. Manson, Alan Richardson and H. E. W. Turner. It is a much more satisfactory view, for it does interpret the miracles in biblical categories, and it can claim the support of Jesus himself, as his teaching is recorded in the gospels (Matt. 11.2-6 par.). It is, however, open to a serious objection. It is becoming increasingly clear[1] that Jesus never used Messianic titles of himself, and that explicit faith in Jesus as Messiah arose only after the resurrection. This does not mean that this belief is contrary to Jesus' intention or to the character of his ministry. Rather, his Messiahship was the *indirect* implication of all he said and did. For all the Messianic titles mean just this: that God was in Christ, present and active and redeeming. There can be no doubt that this is how Jesus understood himself and his mission. His Messiahship is to be sought, not in his explicit use of Messianic titles (this was the work of the post-resurrection church, which transformed its tradition of Jesus' sayings and memory of his doings in the light of its new faith), but in the *content* of what he said

[1] See e.g. G. Bornkamm, *Jesus of Nazareth* (London and New York, 1960).

and did. His Messiahship is to be found in his message that the reign of God is dawning; in his call, 'Follow Me'; in his gracious acceptance of publicans and sinners; in his healings and exorcisms; and finally in his willing exposure of himself to rejection and death at Jerusalem in order to confront Israel with God's last word. In all these activities, Jesus confronts us with 'God's presence and his very self'. Here is the substance of Messiahship: the titles come after the resurrection as the church's believing response. As we shall see in the next chapter, Jesus connected his healings and exorcisms not with an explicit assertion of his Messianic claim but with his message that the Reign of God was dawning in his own activity. This view is thoroughly consistent with the biblical conception of miracle as the intervening action of God. The third chapter will show how Jesus' own interpretation was, quite naturally, reformulated by the church after the resurrection in terms of its own faith in Jesus' Messiahship.

Biblical Words for 'Miracles'

Before we bring this introductory chapter to a close, let us take a brief look at the biblical words used for miracles.

In the Hebrew Old Testament, the most characteristic word is *ôth* (sign). This is the word used of the plagues of Egypt (Exod. 7.3). It need not be, though it often is, an extraordinary event. It suggests an occurrence pointing beyond itself to some further meaning, as the plagues of Egypt pointed forward to the supreme miracle of the Exodus. Since its meaning is not immediately obvious, it represents a challenge to faith. In the Greek New Testament, the corresponding word is *semeion*. In the synoptic gospels, *semeion* has rather a bad meaning. Jesus consistently refuses to give a *semeion*. Here it means a legitimating sign. But the fourth gospel reverts to its Old Testament meaning of a God-given sign pointing beyond itself to a supreme miracle, in this case the cross and resurrection. Also, in the fourth gospel the signs are startlingly miraculous, which they are not necessarily in the Old Testament. Here the Johannine usage is probably influenced by the meaning of *semeion* in paganism, where it usually implies a stupendous miracle. We find the same usage in Acts 4.22, where it means miracle pure and simple, in this context a miraculous healing.

In the synoptic gospels the most important word for miracle is 'mighty work' (Greek: *dunamis*), a word suggested already by the Hebrew Old Testament word *geburah*, but also firmly established in pagan usage. Its meaning in the gospels, however, is different from its pagan sense, for it suggests an act of God who *can* (Greek: *dunatai*) do all things, who is the source of all power.

In addition to *semeion*, another favourite word for miracle in the fourth gospel is 'work' (Greek: *ergon*). It also occurs in one significant passage in Matthew (11.2). Here is another pagan word for miracle. In John it is connected with the Evangelist's profound doctrine of the person of Christ, while the 'signs' foreshadow the great *work* of salvation accomplished on the cross (see especially 9.3). They bear witness to Jesus (10.25) and to his unity with the Father. In fact, Jesus works *are* the works of the Father (14.10).

Occasionally we find the term 'wonder' (Greek: *teras*; cf. Hebrew *mopheth*). The synoptic gospels avoid this word: John uses it once (4.48) in a context with *semeion* in the same depreciatory sense in which the latter is used in the synoptics. 'Wonders' are precisely what it is wrong to look for. It is a common word in paganism for a portent or prodigy. Acts 2.22 uses it in combination with 'sign', both words in a positive sense. Used in combination, the two words lose their questionable character. It is not the miraculous in itself, but the significance of the miracle which is the concern of the biblical writers.

Three other words, all of them found in pagan usage are: 'wonderful things' (Greek: *thaumasia*, Matt. 21.15 only); 'strange things' (Greek *paradoxa*, Luke 5.26 only); 'wonderful deeds' (Greek: *aretai*, I Pet. 2.9 only).

It will be seen at once from this survey that the Bible has no distinctive word of its own for miracle. What is distinctive about the Bible is the way it uses these various terms. Words like *semeion*, *dunamis* and *ergon* are frequent and can be given theological meaning. The more obviously sensational words like *terata*, *thaumasia*, *paradoxa* and *aretai* are rare. It is the association of miracle with the biblical view of God and the world which gives the biblical words for miracle their distinctive character.

2

THE MIGHTY WORKS OF JESUS

Did Jesus Do Miracles?

BEFORE WE try to find out how Jesus understood his miracles, we must ask whether he did them. Are the miracles of Jesus related in the synoptic gospels genuine? Or are they products of Christian faith—credulity, if you will? Many scholars nowadays would bypass the whole question. All we can know, they tell us, is that miracles are part of the apostolic witness to Christ, and you cannot get back behind that witness. Quite frankly, this is not quite honest. After all, the Christian gospel claims that in the *history* of Jesus of Nazareth God has acted finally for man's salvation. The Christian faith involves a specific interpretation of a historical fact, or of a series of historical facts. We have a right to know just what that particular history was. Nor need we be too pessimistic. Modern scholarship has given us the tools which promise fair to help us in that quest. We cannot, of course, prove by the historical method that Jesus' history is the redemptive act of God. That always rests on the decision of faith.

Did Jesus do miracles? Conservative apologists argue like this: 'God can do miracles: Jesus was God incarnate; therefore, he must have been able to do miracles; therefore he did them.' Like so many syllogisms, however, this argument puts the cart before the horse. It rests on an *a priori* assumption which should be a conclusion. That Jesus is God incarnate is a decision made by faith *after* it has been confronted by the history of Jesus, not an assumption to be made *before* we approach that history.

It is equally *a priori* to rule out the miracles from the start as the rationalists did. Miracles, they said, cannot happen. They are scientifically impossible in a universe governed by the cast-iron laws of cause and effect. Therefore, Jesus never did any miracles. They are either misunderstandings of what actually happened or pious legends. The first explanation was beloved of the earlier rationalists. The story of the Gadarene swine, e.g., was originally quite a natural occurrence. The shrieks of the demoniac terrified the swine and caused a panic. As a result some fell over the precipice and the rest followed. In the feeding of the five thousand all that really happened was that the disciples persuaded a young lad to share his sandwiches with others. The idea caught on and everyone else shared their sandwiches until the whole crowd had been fed. That kind of rationalism is now out of fashion. Instead it is now suggested that legends from outside sources have crept into the gospels. The Gadarene swine, for instance, is a local tale which attached itself to Jesus, while the changing of the water into wine was originally a 'cult myth' of the wine-god Dionysus.

Today many would agree with the scholars whose views we described in the previous chapter and accept the healings and exorcisms, while questioning the nature miracles. While the former can be explained psychologically, the nature miracles appear to be ruled out by the scientific world-view.

All these arguments, for or against the genuineness of the recorded miracles, are *a priori* ones. Basically, this is a historical question, and can only be answered by the canons of historical criticism. What we must do is to lay aside, so far as possible, all preconceived notions about the possibility or impossibility of miracles and study the traditions recorded in the gospels to see how far back we can trace them—whether we can take them back to Jesus himself. Above all, we must remember that the cast-iron law of cause and effect, while an indispensable working hypothesis for the scientist, is no more than a hypothesis, and in this connection the scientist ought not to be allowed to dictate to the historian in advance of what the results of his investigation should be. If we find the results of historical criticism conflict with the modern scientific world view we ought in principle to be ready to widen our world view to make room for those results.

Miracles outside the Gospels

Since Jesus never wrote anything we have no first-hand testimony from him. But the Apostle Paul speaks of his own miraculous activity. Writing to the Corinthians, he says:

> The signs of a true apostle were performed among you in all patience, with signs and wonders, and mighty works (II Cor. 12.12).

Again, writing a little later to the Romans, who had not seen him, he says:

> I will not venture to speak of anything except what Christ has wrought through me to win obedience

from the Gentiles, by word and deed, by power or signs and wonders (Rom. 15.18-19a).

Among the gifts of the spirit Paul lists in I Cor. 12 are 'gifts of healing' (v. 9) and the 'working of miracles' (v. 10). He speaks also of similar phenomena in the churches of Galatia (Gal. 3.5).

In addition, we have the secondary evidence of Acts. There is the story of the raising of Eutychus by Paul (Acts 20.7 ff.); the stories about Paul's healing of a lame man at Lystra (Acts 14.8 ff.) and of Publius' father from dysentery (Acts 28.8; other healings follow). Thus on his own showing, confirmed by the secondary evidence of Acts, Paul and his converts could and did heal by extraordinary, non-medical means. If they could do it, there is no reason why Jesus should not have done so, too.

Nor are such healings confined to early Christianity. There are stories in late Judaism which tell of Rabbis who performed 'miraculous' cures. Many such stories were collected together and published in a German translation by a German scholar, Paul Fiebig, in 1911.[1] The best known, perhaps, is the healing of the son of Rabbi Johanan ben Zaccai by Rabbi Hanina ben Dosa. Both Rabbis lived in Palestine *c.* 70 AD, and were therefore almost contemporary with Jesus.

> And again it happened concerning Rabbi Hanina ben Dosa that he went to study the law with Rabbi Johanan ben Zaccai. And the son of Rabbi Johanan ben Zaccai was sick. Then he (i.e. Johanan ben Zaccai) said to him: 'Hanina, my son, pray for mercy for him, that he may live.' Then he (i.e. Hanina) laid

[1] Paul Fiebig, *Jüdische Wundergeschichten des neutestamentlichen Zeitalters* (Tübingen, 1911).

his head between his knees (a posture of earnest prayer) and prayed for mercy for him, and he remained alive (lit. 'he lived').

Then said Rabbi ben Zaccai: 'If ben Zaccai had laid his head between his knees all day they (a phrase meaning 'God') would have taken no notice of him.' Then said his wife to him: 'Is Hanina then greater than you?' Then said he to her: 'No, but he is like a servant before the king, while I am like a prince before the king.'[1]

Further afield, there are the inscriptions discovered on the six pillars at Epidaurus, the Lourdes of the ancient world. Some of the miracles there recorded are fantastic, like the one about the woman who after five years' pregnancy gave birth to a four-year-old child. But others seem quite plausible and may be genuine. Here is an example:

Demosthenes from X, lame in the legs. He came into the shrine on a stretcher and went about supported with canes. As he lay down to sleep (a regular healing technique at Epidaurus), he saw a vision. He dreamed that God ordered him to spend four months in the shrine because in that time he would be healed. Thereupon, within four months, entering the sanctuary during the last days with two canes, he came out healed. (H 64)[2]

The evidence from Paul and the healing miracles outside the Bible make it reasonable to suppose that Jesus too performed miraculous healings. Is there any evidence outside the Bible that he actually did so? The Slavonic version of the history of the Jewish war by

[1] *Bab. Berakoth* 34, from Fiebig's German translation.

[2] Quoted from Lawrence J. McGinley, S.J., *Form-criticism of the Synoptic Healing Narratives* (Woodstock, Md., 1944).

Josephus[1] contains the statement that 'he (Jesus) worked miracles, wonderful and mighty'. This part of Josephus is a mediaeval interpolation. But does it, as some hold, contain an authentic nucleus derived from an early Aramaic source? This is extremely doubtful. And even if we think otherwise, what independent source value has it? It could just as well reflect Christian tradition. The Slavonic Josephus is therefore best left out of account.

More reliable is the Rabbinic tradition in *Tractate Sanhedrin* 43a:

> On the eve of Passover they hanged Yeshu (of Nazareth) and the herald went before him for forty days saying: 'Yeshu of Nazareth is going forth to be stoned in that he hath practised sorcery and beguiled and led astray Israel. Let everyone knowing ought in His defense come and plead for him.' But they found naught in his defence and hanged him on the eve of the Passover.[2]

Many, though not all, scholars would ascribe independent source value to this tradition. 'Practised sorcery' is not the way Christians spoke of their master's miracles. The phrase seems an independent reminiscence of the charge that Jesus was in league with Beelzebul (Mark 3.22; Matt. 12.24, 27). If so, the Jewish tradition supports the claim that Jesus performed exorcisms. Apart from this there is no other external evidence of any kind, no inscriptions for example, such as those at Epidaurus.

[1] In the interpolation between *Antiquities* ii, 174 and 175, entitled 'The Ministry, Trial and Crucifixion of the Wonder-worker'.

[2] Quoted from Joseph Klausner, *Jesus of Nazareth* (New York, 1949).

The Gospels' Witness to Jesus as Miracle-worker

So we are thrown back on the gospels themselves. There is no guarantee that any of the stories recorded in the gospels come directly from eye-witnesses. They passed through oral tradition for at least thirty years before they were written down. The traditional apostolic authorship of the first and fourth gospels is now generally abandoned. Neither author was a follower of Jesus. Even the tradition never claimed direct eye-witness for Mark and Luke, and Luke himself in his preface expressly disclaims it (Luke 1.1-4). But source and form criticism have between them given us tools which help us to get back behind the written gospels and study the growth of the tradition in its earlier stages.

As the reader is probably aware, it is generally agreed that Mark is our oldest gospel, and that Matthew and Luke are basically expansions of Mark. This means that any material which occurs in all three gospels is found in its earliest form in Mark. Matthew's and Luke's alterations to Mark are important clues to their own theology, but are rarely of direct historical value. Matthew and Luke also used another common source, apparently unknown to Mark, at least in the form in which the two later evangelists knew it. The reconstruction of this source is largely a matter of guess-work. We do not even know whether it all came from a single document. Some of it, indeed, was probably not written down at all, but came to both Matthew and Luke from oral tradition—from the preaching and teaching of the primitive Church. This material is commonly called 'Q'. In addition, both Matthew and Luke have special material of their own. Whether this too was derived from written documents is highly uncertain, and the question can only be left open. Thus we have four primary layers of material: Mark, 'Q', special Matthean material, and special Lucan material. Behind each of these layers lies a period of oral transmission, when the stories about Jesus and his saying were used for preaching and teaching.

With the exception of the special Matthean material,[1] all of these strata contain references to Jesus' healings. Mark[2] contains twelve stories of healing (not counting the one raising from the dead), four generalized summaries of the healing ministry and four other allusions to healing or exorcism. Q contains one healing and three other sayings referring to healing or exorcism. The special Lucan material contains two sayings of Jesus which refer to miraculous activity: (*a*) the exorcisms of his disciples (Luke 10.17-20); (*b*) a generalized statement about his own ministry (Luke 13.32). In addition, Special Luke gives three new healings: the bent woman, the dropsical man and the ten lepers. The restoration of the high priest's servant's ear (Luke 22.51) is probably a touch added by the evangelist himself.

Of all this evidence the most valuable is the reference to exorcisms and healings in Jesus' own words. If these sayings are authentic, they contain pretty nearly first-hand evidence that Jesus did perform miracles. The Beelzebul saying is the best attested, since it occurs in Q and is supported indirectly by the Marcan tradition.

[1] The miracles in Matt. 9.27-31; 9.32-34; 12.22 appear to be editorial compositions. So are the generalized summaries at 14.14; 19.2; 21.14-17.

[2] See Index.

The Q Saying

But if it is by the Spirit (Luke: finger) of God that I cast out demons, then the kingdom of God has come upon you. (Matt. 12.27=Luke 11.19)

Mark's indirect support

1. *Narrative material.* And the scribes who came down from Jerusalem said, 'He is possessed by Beelzebul, and by the prince of demons he casts out demons.' (Mark 3.22)

2. *An isolated saying* How can Satan cast out Satan? (Mark 3.23)

When a tradition about Jesus is found in both Mark and Q, it is an early and good tradition which was probably current already during the forties of the first century. But is it any older? Can it be safely said to go back to Jesus himself? Here source criticism can no longer help us, and we have to seek the help of form criticism: the study of the *form* of a gospel passage.[1] This provides us with two criteria to help us to decide whether a saying of Jesus is authentic. (1) If it reflects the faith of the church after the resurrection, it must be regarded as a creation of the church, rather than an authentic saying of Jesus. (2) If there is a parallel saying attributed to a Rabbi, it must be held as a Jewish tradition which has erroneously been attributed to Jesus. But if it is neither—if it is clearly distinct both from the faith of the church and from Judaism—then it may be safely

[1] For accounts of form criticism in general see V. Taylor, *The Formation of the Gospel Tradition* (London, 1933) and E. B. Redlich, *Form Criticism* (London, 1939). Two major works by pioneer form critics are: M. Dibelius, *From Tradition to Gospel* (London, 1933) and Rudolf Bultmann, *The History of the Synoptic Tradition* (Oxford, 1962).

accepted as authentic. If in addition it has a Palestinian flavour and the characteristics of Aramaic speech, this would be additional confirmation of its authenticity. By themselves these last two criteria are insufficient, since the creations of the earliest Palestinian church would naturally have the same characteristics.

Applying these tests to the Q saying which we are studying (Matt. 12.27 par.[1]), we find that it does not reflect the faith of the church, for it makes no explicit assertion that Jesus is Messiah. Moreover, it speaks of the Reign of God as already in some sense breaking in. So it is completely different from anything one would expect from Judaism, where the Kingdom of God was a purely future expectation. Therefore, it is not a saying which has been attributed to Jesus by the church. We may safely assume that it is a genuine saying of Jesus himself.

Next, there is the answer to John:

The blind receive their sight
    and the lame walk,
lepers are cleansed
    and the deaf hear,
and the dead are raised up,
    and the poor have good news preached to them.
And blessed is he who is not offended in me.
(Matt. 11. 4b-6; Luke 7.22 f.: Q.)

This saying is not quite so well attested as the Beelzebul saying, for there is no parallel in Mark. We are therefore thrown back on the tests of form criticism. On the one hand, this saying clearly differs from anything possible in contemporary Judaism. The salvation

[1] I.e., with its parallel in Luke.

of the last day is already in process. To that extent it is characteristic of Jesus. But does it reflect the later church's faith in Jesus as Messiah? At first sight it appears to, for the last line, 'blessed is he who is not offended in me' connects the miracles to the *person* of Jesus. But this is not the *explicit* Christology of the post-Easter church. It refers not to Jesus' role as Messiah, but to his message, and to himself as the bearer of that message, so there is no reason why this too should not be an authentic saying of Jesus.

The third saying is 'The Blessedness of the Disciples':

Blessed are the eyes which see what you see,
    And the ears which hear what you hear;
For I tell you
    that many prophets and kings desired to see what you see,
    and did not see it;
    and to hear what you hear,
    and did not hear it.[1]

Here is the same strong consciousness of fulfilment which is lacking in Judaism and characteristic of Jesus, and the same absence of the explicit Christology of the post-resurrection church. The saying, therefore, satisfies the form-critics' criteria of authenticity.[2] As in the answer to John, the things 'seen' must surely be Jesus' healings or exorcisms.[3]

[1] The version of the saying given here is a reconstruction combining features of both Luke 10.24 and Matt. 13.16-17.

[2] Note also the poetic structure (parallelism) characteristic of Aramaic verse.

[3] The woes on the Galilean cities (also Q) might also be cited, but they are not so certainly authentic.

When Jesus sends out his disciples on a mission he commands them, either directly or indirectly, to heal the sick and cast out evil spirits (see Mark 3.14 f.; Luke 10.9 par.: Q). That he should have done so is further confirmation of his having performed such things himself.

Finally, there is a saying from the special Lucan material:

> Go, and tell that fox,
> 'Behold, I cast out demons
> and perform cures
> today and tomorrow' (Luke 13.32).

Although there are difficulties about the whole saying of which this is a part, this part of it is generally accepted as authentic.[1] Jesus here regards his ministry of healing as his most important work.

The evidence in favour of the general tradition of Jesus' exorcisms is little short of overwhelming. It is attested by a Jewish source, and by both of the earliest strata in the synoptic gospels (Mark and Q). The evidence for the other cures is slightly less strong, for there is no Jewish support. Some have suggested that all of the healings were originally exorcisms, and certainly there are traces of the treatment of healings as exorcisms. This is certainly a possibility. Otherwise, we must say that the evidence in favour of the healings, if not quite so overwhelming, is very strong.

Healings and Exorcisms

But granted that the general tradition is reliable, what

[1] See my discussion in *The Mission and Achievement of Jesus*, pp. 62 ff. Günther Bornkamm, *Jesus of Nazareth*, p. 154, also accepts it.

about the actual *stories* of Jesus' miraculous healing? Are they genuine memories of actual miracles Jesus did?

Here source criticism cannot help us, for the miracle stories all rest upon the evidence of a single primary source (Mark or Special Luke). There are, for instance, no miracle stories recorded in *both* Mark *and* Q. We are therefore obliged to seek the help of form criticism, which seeks to throw light on the transmission of these stories in the oral tradition before they were written down in the primary sources. This method of study seeks first to classify the units of material from which the primary sources were composed; secondly, to determine the creative *milieu*—the activity in the life of the early church—in which these units of material took shape; and thirdly, to decide on the historical value of these traditions.

Applying these enquiries to the miracle stories, the form critics distinguish between two types: those in which the miracle merely provides the setting for a significant saying of Jesus (we shall call these 'pronouncement stories'), and those in which the miracle itself provides the climax. The miracles of the synoptic gospels are listed in the Index.

With regard to the pronouncement stories, the form critics are not agreed as to the creative *milieu* in which they took shape. Some would say it was in the preaching of the Greek-speaking communities outside of Palestine, others that it was in the debates of the Palestine church with the Pharisees. This in turn leads to a difference in the answer they give to the third question, whether the stories are genuine or not. Those who think that preaching was their creative *milieu* incline to the view that the incident which provides the setting for the saying rests upon genuine memory, while those who think that the debates with the Pharisees provided the creative *milieu* hold the reverse opinion, namely that the saying is likely to be authentic, while the setting is an 'ideal scene' constructed as a carrier for the saying.

With regard to the miracle stories proper, the form critics agree that the creative *milieu* for them was the Greek-speaking Christian communities outside Palestine. As for the activity which led to the creation of these stories, some hold that there was a class of story-tellers in these churches, who told them either for sheer entertainment—the early Christians could not borrow novels from the local library!—or as recipes for the church to copy in its own ministry of healing. Others have called attention to the similarity of the gospel stories to those found in the religious literature of paganism in the Graeco-Roman world. Such stories are completely absent from the Rabbinic literature, which would seem to suggest that these gospel miracles could not have originated in Palestine. The pagan parallels, however, do not necessarily imply direct borrowing on the part of the Greek-speaking Christians: they merely show the kind of atmosphere in which the Christian stories arose. Since they are agreed that the miracle stories proper arose in the Greek-speaking churches outside Palestine, the form critics also agree that they have little or no historical value.

Can we arrive at a judgement of our own? That the 'pronouncement stories' come from the Palestinian churches is clear. They are obviously concerned with issues which were acute in Palestine, such as the keeping of the sabbath. But there is more to be said than has been commonly allowed for the view that the miracles which provided the setting in these stories are 'ideal scenes', deliberately created to carry the saying. After all, the church was interested in the saying, not in the setting. Sometimes, too, it is quite clear that the scene has been deliberately created, as in the case of the dumb demoniac which Matthew has created to carry the Beelzebul sayings handed down without any setting by Mark and Q (Matt. 12.22 par.). If this happened in one instance, it probably happened in others as well.

But were these 'ideal scenes' created out of nothing? Is it not more likely that the early Christians drew upon their store of *generalized memory* about Jesus? If these stories originated in the Palestinian community, this is more than likely. The dumb demoniac, the withered hand, the bent woman, and the dropsical man—all of these will not be stories of what Jesus actually did on a specific occasion, but will represent the *kind* of thing he used to do. Yet we would not rule out the possibility that occasionally a *specific* memory of an actual incident has been preserved. Certain features of the narrative make this likely in the case of the paralytic, the Syrophoenician woman and the centurion of Capernaum. This does not mean that the healings in question took place exactly as narrated; the miracle stories are not like evidence given in a court of law. But it does mean that there is some factual basis to them. One more pronouncement story needs to be accounted for, the Special Lucan ten lepers. This has perhaps been developed out of Mark's story of the leper. We can easily see how this could have happened in the hands of some Christian preacher who wished to bring out a new point from the story.

What, next, of the form critics' judgement on the

miracle stories proper? To claim that they all originated in the later communities outside Palestine is too sweeping. The argument from the similarity of pattern between the gospel stories and pagan legends is not really so conclusive as it sounds. Let us examine the pattern. It is threefold:

(1) *Setting* (description of the illness; its length, previous failures of physicians to cure).
(2) *Cure* (the technique—a word, gesture or application of physical means; the cure performed secretly).
(3) *Demonstration* (the reality of the cure attested by an action of the patient or by the attestation of the witnesses; frequently by a 'choric ending').

Two points must be made here. First the threefold pattern is not confined to the ancient pagan world. It tends to reproduce itself the world over. Dibelius himself notes a modern parallel from Lourdes, and another German scholar has even produced one from Frankfurt-am-Main. Canon H. E. W. Turner has said that one doctor's case book must look very much like another's while the late Bishop Kirk once discovered the same threefold pattern in a modern cartoon advertisement for Ovaltine! Reports of cures seem inevitably to fall into this threefold pattern. Nor is it surprising that such stories are lacking in Rabbinic Judaism. Rabbinic healings are occasional incidents performed in answer to prayer, not characteristic activities of their ministry. Given the basic fact that Jesus did perform healings and exorcisms, the stories about his deeds would naturally fall into this pattern, whether in the Palestinian or the Hellenistic (Greek-speaking) communities. Also, there are in the gospels very few pure miracle stories of the type found in the Hellenistic world. There is nearly always some specifically Christian interest at work, such as the theme of faith, or Jesus' Messiahship. This results in a disruption of the conventional pattern by the introduction of dialogues between Jesus and the patient or his friends.

Another point is that there are a number of miracle stories whose language seems to indicate that they were first told in Aramaic. These include the Capernaum demoniac, the Gerasene demoniac (the incident of the swine may well be a local yarn tacked on later as an afterthought) and the woman with the haemorrhage. The epileptic boy looks like a combination of two stories, one which contrasts the apprentices and the master wonder-worker (Mark 9.20, 28 f.), another which centres upon the paradox of unbelieving faith as shown by the boy's father (vv. 21-27). The first story is paralleled in Hellenistic literature, and it may well have been added later by the Greek-speaking Christians outside Palestine, while the second story may well be an earlier (Aramaic) tradition.

Only three miracle stories exhibit the pure form of a Hellenistic wonder story, without any modification: Peter's mother-in-law, the deaf mute and the blind man of Bethsaida. The first of these, however, is undoubtedly a personal reminiscence of Peter himself.[1] The others are the only cases in the synoptic tradition where Jesus uses spittle. There is a similar story of the Emperor Vespasian's cure of a blind man by the same technique. It does look as though these two stories entered in the tradition from a popular source outside Palestine in the

[1] See R. H. Lightfoot, *The Gospel Message of St Mark* (Oxford, 1950), p. 22.

Greek-speaking world. It is interesting, and perhaps significant, that Matthew omits them both.

Apart from these two isolated instances, and apart from the later additions to the Gerasene demoniac and the epileptic boy, the miracle stories appear to be no less Palestinian in origin than the pronouncement stories. Most of them also appear to rest on generalized memory. The Capernaum demoniac, the leper, the paralytic (Mark 2.1-12; originally minus vv. 6-10), the Gerasene demonaic (minus the swine), the woman with the haemorrhage, and the epileptic boy (minus the part about the disciples), represent the *kind* of things Jesus did rather than what he actually did on those occasions. In two cases, however, the memory seems specific rather than general: Simon's mother-in-law (see above) and blind Bartimaeus, who has the distinction of being the only patient named in the early tradition.[1] He followed Jesus in the *way* (Mark 10.52). That suggests that he was a disciple and a well-known member of the Christian community like Alexander and Rufus (Mark 15.21). So this story may well rest on a specific memory.

Another type of passage in St Mark's gospel which mentions healings and exorcisms is the generalized summaries (see Index). A careful examination of the language of these summaries suggests that they are composed by the evangelist from details in the miracle stories.[2] In spite of their late origin, however, these

[1] The naming of Jairus is almost certainly due to Luke: in Mark 5.22 the probable text omits the name. Normally the tendency is for names to come in as the tradition grows.

[2] Compare, for example, the language of Mark 3.11 with 1.23 f.; 5.7 and with 9.26; the cry of the demons in the same verse with 2.7; also the 'pallet beds' of 6.55 with 2.4; and the touching of the hem of Jesus' garment in 6.56 with 5.28.

summaries are valuable as supplementary testimony to the general tradition. They show that the separate stories which have been preserved are only a selection from a larger body of memories. They also have a negative value, for they contain no raisings from the dead and no nature miracles. This suggests that even if Jesus did perform miracles of that type, they were highly exceptional, not regular features of his ministry.

Raisings from the dead are mentioned in the answer to John (Q), which as we have seen, is undoubtedly authentic. Most of the answer to John is based on the Messianic prophecies of Isaiah (29.18 f.; 35. 5 f.; Isa. 61.1). Only two phrases do not come from Isaiah: the cleansing of the lepers and the raising of the dead. The lepers are clearly taken not from prophecy, but from fact. Is the same true of the raising of the dead? Possibly, yet Jesus *can* speak of the 'dead' in a figurative sense: 'Let the dead bury their dead' (Matt. 8.22 par.: Q). So we cannot be sure whether the answer to John should be taken as evidence from Jesus' own lips that he actually raised the dead.

The two narratives of raisings (Jairus' daughter in Mark and the widow's son at Nain in Luke) are assigned by the form critics to the Hellenistic churches. The language of both stories, however, is remarkably Hebraic, and they may well go back to the Palestinian church. Those who take the answer to John literally will feel that both these raisings go back to genuine memories. If we take the answer to John figuratively, we shall want to account for the rise of the two stories differently. In that case, Jairus' daughter was not originally dead, *but only on the point of death* (Mark

5.23),[1] while the widow's son at Nain could have been modelled on the raisings of Elijah and Elisha in II Kings.

Nature Miracles

No New Testament writer would have thought of putting the 'nature miracles' in a separate class. But they do make a difference, perhaps unconsciously, between the nature miracles, and the healings and exorcisms. For the disciples are the only people to witness them. This is really true even of the feeding of the multitude: there is no suggestion that the crowd knew what had happened, any more than the guests at the marriage of Cana knew. The early church did not regard the nature miracles as a feature of Jesus' *public* ministry.

Since the feeding of the multitude occupies such a clearly defined place at a critical turn of the ministry we may reasonably suppose that it grew out of a genuine memory. What actually happened can no longer be recovered, for the story as told in the gospels has been shaped by later theology: ideas of the Messianic banquet, the manna in the wilderness, and the miraculous plenty of the Messianic age.

The miraculous draft of fishes, as St John's version (21.1 ff.) and sundry features in Luke's account[2] suggest, was originally a resurrection appearance. It has been placed where it is in Luke to illustrate the saying, 'I will make you fishers of men'.

The walking on the water may have developed from

[1] Cf. also the centurion's boy in Q—Matt. 8, Luke 7—and the official's son in John 4.46-53, possibly variants of the same story.

[2] See my *Luke's Witness to Jesus Christ* (London and New York, 1958), p. 26.

the stilling of the storm (see Mark 6.48, 51). Both traditions may therefore rest on the same historical reminiscence, though precisely what happened can no longer be recovered, for they have been overlaid by theological motives (see below, pp. 53 f., 58 f.).

Canon Turner has suggested[1] that the nature miracles should be relegated to a 'theological suspense account'. But it is not the theology of the nature miracles which is in question. The real problem is, did they happen? So why not put them into a *historical* suspense account? At all events, we must avoid *a priori* judgements either for or against them. What really gives us grounds for doubt is their theological colouring and the absence of any allusion to nature miracles in Q and indeed, anywhere in the recorded sayings of our Lord.

Let us take an example. Did Jesus actually curse the fig tree? It certainly seems out of character, for his other miracles all have a positive purpose—to make people well. That is why so many modern scholars have welcomed the theory that this story is really developed from a parable (see Luke 13.6 ff.). It has also been suggested (without evidence) that the story arose from a withered tree which was a well-known landmark outside Jerusalem. Yet some people do apparently have a power to curse things effectively. (The late Archbishop Lang once cursed a new hotel which had been built on a loch where he used to fish—and it burnt down a week or two after!) So no one can say Jesus could not have cursed the fig tree. But since it occurs in only one primary document it is not well attested. The rarity of nature miracles, their absence from Q, from

[1] H. E. W. Turner, *Jesus, Master and Lord* (London and New York, 1954), p. 181.

other sayings of Jesus and from Mark's summaries and the fact that only the disciples witness them, throw serious doubt on their having happened exactly as they are recorded. We think that there is probably some historical basis for some of them, for traditions are rarely created out of nothing. All we can safely say is that they probably came into the tradition somewhat later than the healings and exorcisms.

To sum up, then: while the tradition that Jesus did perform exorcisms and healings (which may also have been exorcisms originally) is very strong, we can never be certain of the authenticity of any actual miracle story in the gospels. While a few of them may rest upon specific memory, most of them have probably been shaped out of generalized memories.

Jesus Interprets His Miracles

That Jesus performed healings and exorcisms is not incredible. First-hand evidence of such phenomena in the apostolic church and the Jewish and pagan parallels make them plausible. The modern reader can, if he wishes, attribute them to the natural effect of Jesus' personality upon the sick, an explanation which becomes all the more credible in the light of modern psychosomatic medicine.

This means, however, that the miracles of Jesus were not unique. Jesus himself recognized this, at least in the case of the exorcisms: 'If I cast out demons by Beelzebul, by whom do your sons cast them out?' (Matt. 12.27 par.: Q). If there is anything unique about them it lies not in the miracles themselves, but in *Jesus' understanding of them*. In the very next verse he sharply distinguishes between the meaning of the exorcisms performed by others and of those performed by himself: 'But if it is by the Spirit (Luke: finger) of God that *I* (this I is emphatic) cast out demons, then the kingdom of God has come upon you' (Matt. 12.28 par.: Q).

Jesus' exorcisms are closely connected with his message of the dawning Reign of God.[1] They are not the works of a human wonder-worker, but acts of the Spirit or finger of God, direct acts of God himself, foreshadowing the establishment of his final Reign in the last days. In other words, they are precisely *miracles* in the *biblical* sense of the word (see above, pp. 8 ff.). This saying does not appear in Mark's version of the Beelzebul controversy, but he does preserve a similar saying:

> How can Satan cast out Satan? If a kingdom is divided against itself, that kingdom cannot stand. And if a house is divided against itself, that house will not be able to stand. And if Satan has risen up against himself and is divided, he cannot stand, but is coming to an end. But no one can enter a strong man's house and plunder his goods, unless he first binds the strong man; then indeed he may plunder his house (Mark 3.23b-27).

Jesus interprets his exorcisms as the beginning of the end of Satan's reign. Here again, as in Q, the exorcisms are set in the context of the coming of the Reign of God. And since it is God's own prerogative to establish his kingly rule, this again implies that Jesus' exorcisms are not the acts of a human wonder-worker, but the direct acts of God himself. Once more, too, the exor-

[1] For a discussion of the concept of the Reign of God, see my *The Mission and Achievement of Jesus*, pp. 20-49.

cisms are preliminary in character: the 'first' binding of the strong man before the plundering of his house.[1] The final coming of the Reign of God still lies in the future: the exorcisms, like the message of Jesus, herald its beginning.

So much for the exorcisms. What of the healings?

The blind receive their sight
Jesus interprets these in the answer to John:
    and the lame walk,
Lepers are cleansed
    and the deaf hear,
And the dead are raised up,
    and the poor have good news preached to them,
And blessed is he who takes no offence at me.
(Matt. 11.5 f. par.: Q.)

This is not a mere enumeration of the healings: it is a description of them in terms derived from Isaiah's prophecies of the age to come.[2] Jesus' activity is a sign of the dawn of the age of salvation, the end-time Reign of God. And the use of the passive ('lepers are cleansed', rather than 'I am cleansing lepers') denotes that the things which are happening are not the works of Jesus himself as a human wonder-worker, but things that God himself is doing through him. Its meaning, rather, is that Jesus' own person is intimately bound up with his proclamation and healings as a sign of the dawning of God. Jesus understands himself as the one in whom God is beginning his saving action. This, of course, *implies* what the church later meant when it called him by the Messianic titles after the resurrection. The substance of

[1] See *op. cit.*, p. 38.
[2] See *op. cit.*, pp. 34 ff.

Messiahship is there, but it is not explicitly claimed. Rather, Jesus points away from himself to God, and to himself only as the one in whom God is beginning his decisive action.

The woes on the Galilean cities (Matt. 11.21-24 par.: Q) give the same interpretation of Jesus' works of power: they are the acts of God (note the word 'done') and they have the same relation to the coming end (note the references to the day of judgement in vv. 22, 24). This saying is not, however, as assuredly authentic as the Beezlebul controversy and the answer to John.

Faith and Miracles

That this is how Jesus understood his exorcisms and healings is confirmed in the part played by *faith* in the gospel narratives. How often in the gospels does Jesus say to the person cured, 'Your faith has made you well' (Mark 5.34; cf. 10.52 par.; Luke 17.19, which is Special Luke)! This saying must surely have been characteristic of Jesus. Mark's frank admission that Jesus 'could do no work of power at Nazareth' (6.5) points in the same direction. 'Faith' does not have the modern sense of 'faith-healing'. Jesus does not heal merely by the power of suggestion. For often the faith in question is the faith of the sick person's relatives (Mark 7.24 ff.) or his friends (Mark 2.3 ff.; Matt. 8.5 ff.), and there are cases of healing from a distance (Mark 7.24 ff., Matt 8.5 ff.). Nor is it merely faith in Jesus as a wonder-worker, as in the pagan miracle stories. Faith in the gospels is directed, not to Jesus himself as a wonder-worker, but to the power of God active in him. Faith is the proper human attitude at the receiving end of an act of God. It is closely connected in Jesus' teaching with prayer, which looks to a responding action of God, and has power to call forth that act:

> Have faith in God. [Note: Jesus does not demand faith in himself.] Truly I say to you, whoever says to this mountain, 'Be taken up and cast into the sea,' and does not doubt in his heart, but believes that what he says will come to pass, it will be done [reverential passive = God will do it] for him. (Mark 11.22-25; cf. Matt. 17.20 par.: Q.)

Yet faith, although it is on the receiving end of God's act, is not just a passive attitude. It precedes the act of God and actively seeks his help. It is 'an energetic, importunate, grasping after the help of God'.[1] When Jesus says 'Your faith has made you well' he does not mean merely that the patient has screwed himself up by the power of auto-suggestion to such a pitch that he recovers. Nor on the other hand does he mean that the sick person is purely passive. Faith implies action and reaction between man and God. The sick person energetically grasps God's help, and his importunity, like prayer itself, calls forth an act of God.

We must note also that although this faith is not directly focused upon Jesus himself as a wonder-worker, it is intimately bound to his person, for it is *through him* that the powers of God for salvation are made active. Thus miracle-faith implies once more a Christological estimate of Jesus' person, although it is not explicitly directed to him as Messiah. Only after the resurrection does that happen, and then the miracle stories are naturally reshaped into explicit manifesta-

[1] C. E. B. Cranfield, *Scottish Journal of Theology*, March 1950, p. 66.

tions of Jesus' Messiahship. This is not a corruption of Jesus' understanding of the miracles, so long as we remember that the Messianic titles ascribed to Jesus after the resurrection mean that Jesus is the one in whom *God* has acted decisively for man's redemption, the one in whom God was (and, through the church's preaching of Jesus, is) directly present.

The synoptic gospels frequently refer to Jesus' refusal to provide his critics with 'signs' (Mark 8.11 f. par.; Matt. 12.38 f. par.: Q). In its original form in Mark[1] this refusal is unqualified: 'Truly I say to you, no sign shall be given to this generation.' Jesus consistently refused to perform miracles to prove his own authority, or the truth of his message. The same point lies behind the temptation story (Matt. 4.1 ff. par.), where Jesus refuses to demonstrate his divine sonship by casting himself down from the pinnacle of the Temple. These passages support our contention that Jesus did not understand his works of power as proofs of his Messiahship. In one sense, of course, they were signs—signs of the dawning Reign of God. But they were not *proofs* even of that, for the mighty works are themselves part of the breaking in of the Reign. And if Jesus had offered his miracles as proofs either of his Messiahship or of the coming Reign of God he would have completely contradicted his own conception of faith as free decision rather than coerced opinion.

To sum up, we may say that for Jesus his exorcisms and healings, while not unique in themselves, are unique in their relation to his message of the dawning Reign of God. They constitute a challenge to faith—faith in the

[1] For the originality of the Marcan form, see *The Mission and Achievement of Jesus*, p. 39 f.

redemptive action of God which is breaking through in his person, his words and deeds. But they are not proofs. They summon men to a decision. Those who witness Jesus' exorcisms and healings are perfectly free to decide negatively, to decide that they are done by Beelzebul, the prince of the devils. But they may also decide that they are miracles, wrought by the spirit and finger of God.

3

INTERPRETING THE MIRACLES IN THE PRIMITIVE CHURCH

THE FIRST disciples' encounters with the Risen Lord finally established in them the conviction that Jesus was the one in whom God has decisively acted for man's salvation. This is what they meant by calling Jesus Messiah. This message they proclaimed first to Israel. They organized their converts into a community, and moulded its life in obedience to the will of God revealed in Jesus Christ. It was to further these activities that they recalled the things that Jesus had said and done while he sojourned on earth. These memories were re-shaped in the service of the post-Easter faith of the church, and used in its preaching to the unconverted and in the instruction of the converts.

Included in those memories were the miracles of Jesus. He himself interpreted them as signs of the dawning of the age to come. The early church reinterpreted them as signs that Jesus was Messiah. They were not just relating what had happened in Jesus' earthly life. They were proclaiming what he meant for faith in their own day. They must have known that before his resurrection Jesus had not openly appeared as Messiah (Acts 2.36), but since their concern was not merely to describe what had actually happened in the past, they were not troubled that this reinterpretation was necessary.

We will now analyse the meaning of the miracles in the oral tradition behind our primary sources (Q, Mark and the Special Lucan material). We shall have to use the results of the form-critical work which distinguishes between the original units and the connecting links composed by the evangelists to join these units together. Our concern here is with the miracles as related in oral tradition: with the faith of the church before the gospels were written. The significance of the miracles in the theology of the Evangelists themselves will become important in Chapter 4.

The Tradition in Q

Much of the Q material simply reproduces the actual preaching of Jesus himself. For example, his proclamation of the nearness of God's final reign is taken over as it stands (Matt. 10.7 par.; 11.12 par.). But the Q material also reproduces the church's preaching of Jesus as the Messiah, and reshapes other sayings of Jesus to convey its own proclamation.

This has happened in the answer to John (Matt. 11.2-6 par.). This saying is now prefaced with an introduction: 'John sent disciples to Jesus, saying "Are you the Coming One, or do we look for another?"' (Matt. 11.3 par.). The introduction transforms the answer to John into an explicit declaration of Jesus' Messiahship. The healings and other mighty works performed by Jesus are now signs that *he* is the Coming One. And the final word, 'Blessed is he who takes no offence at me' (Matt. 11.6 par.) now becomes explicitly Messianic. No longer, as in the preaching of Jesus, is a man's status at the last judgement determined by his reaction to Jesus' message of the coming kingdom. It is now determined by his reaction to the *person* of Jesus, whom the church now preaches as the Coming One or Messiah.

There is only one miracle story in the Q material, *the centurion of Capernaum* (Matthew 8.5-13; Luke 7.1-10). Like Mark's account of the Syro-Phoenician woman, it has a missionary motive. It takes seriously the division between Jew and gentile. Jesus is reluctant to break through this barrier, but he does so because of, and only because of, the persistent faith of the centurion. The healing at a distance is perhaps a way of saying that Jesus did not go to the gentiles directly during his earthly ministry; he is now doing it at a distance, from heaven, through his agents on earth.

The point and climax of the story lies in Jesus' pronouncement: 'Truly I say to you, not even in Israel have I found such faith' (Matt. 8.10 par.). Faith here is more than an energetic grasping for the help of God—though it is still that too. It is the centurion's insight that Jesus stands under authority like himself, and therefore, like him, has authority to command. Jesus' authority, present in his word during his ministry on earth, vindicated by the resurrection, present now in the church through the word and sacraments, rests entirely on his authorization by God. Thus he is the channel of the divine action. Here is the beginning of Christological reflection.

The Marcan Material

The Capernaum demoniac (Mark 1.21-28) has features in common with the pagan wonder-stories. There is a brief description of the illness, followed by a cure accomplished by a word of command, 'Be silent [literally: be muzzled] and come out of him', and concluded by an acclamation of the crowd to demonstrate the success of the cure.

The striking and unconventional feature of this story, however, is the way in which the demon addresses Jesus: 'Have you come to destroy us? I know who you are, the Holy One of God.' The demon, belonging to the supernatural world, penetrates Jesus' incognito and perceives him to be the Holy One of God (an early Messianic title; see Acts 3.14) who has come to destroy the kingdom of evil. This story preaches the coming and manifestation of the Messiah.

The cure of *Simon's mother-in-law* (1.29-31) was, as we have seen, a purely historical reminiscence. It contains no saying to give it a theological point: it is simply related because Peter remembered it, and because it was presumably a matter of personal interest to him. There are exceptions to every rule!

The leper (1.40-45) shows many traits of a conventional miracle story. The strong emotion of the wonder-worker is emphasized: Jesus is 'angry'.[1] He heals by a touch. The success of the cure is demonstrated by the command: 'Go show yourself to the priest.' This conventional feature, however, is expanded so as to give theological point to the story: 'and offer for your cleansing what Moses commanded for a witness to them'. Moses made these regulations as an act of wit-

[1] NEB translates v. 41: 'with warm indignation'. The usual reading 'moved with pity' is probably a later modification, and the more difficult reading is to be preferred. The anger of Jesus has been variously explained as due to the leper's breach of the law in seeking out Jesus in a public place, as anger that humanity should be so under the thraldom of evil. The best explanation is that the wonder-worker has to work up his emotions in preparation for the difficult deed of healing, as in John 11.35, 38.

ness to the coming of the Messiah. The scripture has now been fulfilled because Jesus has cleansed this leper. The point is the same as in John 5.45: 'He [Moses] wrote of me.' Jesus is no ordinary human wonder-worker, but the one in whom God fulfils his promises in the Old Testament.

The healing of *the paralytic* (2.1-12) can perhaps be best understood as a combination of two strands of tradition. In its earlier form, it probably did not include 2.6-11, but read as follows:

> And they came bringing to him a paralytic carried by four men. And when they could not get near him because of the crowd, they removed the roof above him; and when they had made an opening, they let down the pallet on which the paralytic lay. And when Jesus saw their faith, he said to the paralytic, 'My son, your sins are forgiven. I say to you, arise, take up your pallet and go home.' And he arose, and immediately took up the pallet and went out before them all, so that they were all amazed, and glorified God, saying, 'We never saw anything like this!'

There are several conventional features in this story. There is an elaborate description of the bringing of the man to Jesus. Its vividness should not be mistaken for a sign of eye-witness: it is simply due to the oriental love of telling a tale. Jesus cures the patient with a word. The reality of the cure is demonstrated by the statement that the man picks up his pallet and goes home, and by the final acclamation of the crowd (v. 12). Again, however, it would be wrong to dismiss this as a mere wonder-story. For it has other features which distinguish it from the pagan parallels. First, Jesus notices their 'faith'. This transforms the elaborate description of the digging through the roof from a picturesque oriental detail into an outward sign of the faith of the paralytic and his friends, their determination to seek help from Jesus. This is faith in its biblical sense, the 'energetic grasping' of the help and power of God. Jesus treats the man's plight not as mere physical illness, but as the symptom of a deeper malady, his sin. He offers him the gift of 'remission'.[1] The healing of the paralysis and the remission of sins are not two separate things, the one inward and spiritual, the other outward and physical. The remission of sins is the total gift of salvation of which physical healing is a part. Finally, the acclamation of the crowd at the end is given a biblical twist: they glorify *God*. In other words, Jesus is the one in whom God acts, not just a human wonder-worker. Here is a profoundly biblical and Christian story and we can easily see how it was used in Christian preaching: God in Christ was still doing in the Christian community through word and sacrament what Jesus did on earth.

The original tale, already modified by these specifically biblical and Christian traits, has, we may suppose, been expanded[2] by the insertion of a debate about Jesus' authority to remit sins:

> SCRIBE: Why does this man speak thus? It is blasphemy! Who can forgive sins, but God alone?

[1] 'Forgive' (RSV and NEB) is a weak translation. Sin is a power which holds man in bondage, and from which Jesus offers release.

[2] It has been asked whether the insertion was the work of the evangelist, or of the tradition before him. Probably the latter; for Mark would never have inserted the Son of man saying (v. 10) at this stage of his narrative. Except at 2.10, 28 (where too it was probably already embedded in the tradition), Mark confines the term Son of man to the period after Caesarea Philippi (8.31).

> JESUS: Why do you question among yourselves? Which is easier, to say to the paralytic, 'Your sins are forgiven' or to say, 'Rise, take up your pallet and walk'? But that you may know that the Son of man has authority on earth to forgive sins (he said to the paralytic) . . .

The punch line in this insertion is the saying, 'The Son of man has authority on earth to remit sins'. The creative *milieu* in which the dialogue took shape is a church which had been charged with blasphemy for dispensing remission of sins in the name of Jesus. It is not the church as a human community which is doing it, but Jesus as Son of man. 'Son of man' does not mean 'man' in the sense of man in general, nor is it simply an equivalent to Jesus' ego. It is definitely Messianic. Jesus is represented here as one who already in his lifetime, and therefore as exalted Son of man in the church, has remitted sins in anticipation of the final remission of sins at the day of judgement. The Christian community derives its authority to remit sins (cf. Luke 10.16 par.; Q; Matt. 16.17-19) from the authority of Jesus as Son of man. The miracles of Jesus have the same meaning as his eating with publicans and tax collectors. They are acts by which he makes available in advance the blessings of the age to come.

The withered hand (3.1-6) is a pronouncement story. The description of the sickness and cure are reduced to a minimum, and all the emphasis is thrown upon the Jesus' question, 'Is it lawful on the sabbath to do good or to do harm, to save life or to kill?' At first sight this looks like a purely humanitarian lesson. But the phrases 'to do good' and 'to save life' are used in a profound, biblical sense. 'Doing good' is the saving action of the

Messiah. In the Old Testament 'good' is often a word for the blessings brought by the exodus from Egypt and God's care of Israel throughout her history (Exod. 18.9; Num. 10.29 ff.; Hos. 8.3; 14.3). Later, it is applied to the blessings of the age to come (Jer. 32.42), a usage which is taken up in the New Testament to define the blessings which have been brought by the advent of the Christ (Heb. 9.11; 10.1). So when we read in Acts 10.38 that Jesus went about doing good and healing, this is not humanitarian, but Messianic action, as it is in the present passage. 'To save life' is clearly the work of the Messiah, while its appropriateness on the sabbath lies in the fact that the sabbath was regarded as a type of prefigurement of the kingdom of God.

The stilling of the storm (4.35-41) is vividly told and full of detail, down to the very cushion on which Jesus was sleeping in the prow of the ship. There is a graphic contrast between the disciples' terror and Jesus' imperturbability, and the words 'there was a great calm' are powerful in their effect. It would be wrong to see here the hand of an eye-witness: it is just the oriental art of story-telling, and shows how close Mark is to the oral tradition. But this is not simply a conventional miracle story. The narrative reaches its climax in the disciples' acclamation at the end, a conventional trait in itself, yet with a biblical twist: 'Who then is this, that even the wind and the sea obey him?' (v. 41). The question is deliberately left unanswered, and points to the Old Testament passages which speak of Yahweh's power to still the raging of the sea:

> who dost still the roaring of the seas
> the roaring of their waves,
> the tumult of the peoples. (Ps. 65.7.)

Then they cried to the Lord in their trouble,
and he delivered them from their distress;
he made the storm be still,
and the waves of the sea were hushed.
(Ps. 107.28 f.)

So, despite the strong affinities between this story and the pagan miracles, it is not just the portrait of a wonder-worker; it is the story of a divine revelation. The power of Yahweh is present in Jesus, as it was in the original act of creation. The chaos of the world[1] is being restored to its pristine order.

The Gerasene demoniac (5.1-20) is equally vivid and is full of typical traits. There is a detailed description of the patient and his illness and of his meeting with Jesus. Like an evil spirit in a Rabbinic story, which asked to be allowed out on sabbaths and Wednesday nights (!), the demon asks to be allowed to stay in the region. Like an exorcised demon in Josephus which smashed a basin full of water, and like a demon in a pagan story which smashed a statue, the demons, when driven out, enter a herd of swine. The terrain is graphically, though not altogether accurately (see the commentaries), described. There is a dramatic contrast between the frenzy of the demoniac, and the cured man 'clothed and in his right mind'. All these features indicate a popular oriental story. But there are other, Christian, traits. The demon's cry makes the story of a manifestation[2] of Jesus as the Son of the Most High God. And it ends on a missionary

[1] Note the details which suggest an exorcism: Jesus 'rebuked' the wind as he rebuked the demons (v. 39; cf. 1.25): 'be muzzled' (RSV 'be still') is the same command as in the exorcisms (1.25).

[2] In the English (not American) BCP it is the gospel for Epiphany IV. In the Epiphany season we read stories of the 'epiphanies' or manifestations of God in Jesus.

note (5.20). At Jesus' command, the man becomes an evangelist and proclaims[1] what God in Christ had done for him. We can imagine such a story taking shape in a district like Decapolis, where converts had a first-hand experience of Jesus' victory over the demon-ridden impurities of pagan living. Let the good news be spread!

It was probably not Mark, but the oral tradition, which inserted the cure of *the woman with the haemorrhage* (5.25-34) into the body of the story of *Jairus' daughter* (5.22-24, 35-43). If the form critics are right, it was done in order to account for Jesus' delay, to explain why the girl was dead by the time he arrived in the house. The delay of the wonder-worker is a common feature in stories of resuscitation (cf. John 11.21). There are other conventional features: the mention of the length of the woman's illness, and of the failure of the doctors to cure her, the touching of the healer's garment without his knowledge, the notion of the healing power as a kind of manna whose loss is physically felt. These are all popular ideas, some of them bordering on the superstitious. In the raising of the little girl the crowd pours scorn on the wonder-worker. The miracle is performed in privacy (cf. Mark 7.33), which adds an air of mystery to the scene. The wonder-worker uses a magic foreign phrase *Talitha, cumi* (cf. *Ephphatha*, Mark 7.34), a sort of conjuror's *Abracadabra*. The girl rises and walks, and Jesus requests that she be given something to eat: these are proofs of the cure. The amazement of the crowd is also typical. But both stories contain features of a very different kind, for despite their affinities with the secular miracle tales they have been

[1] For the word 'tell' in a missionary context compare Acts 15.27; 26.20.

given a distinctively Christian interpretation. The healing of the woman, if it were just a popular tale, should have ended at v. 32, expanded perhaps with an acclamation from the bystanders. Instead, we get the scene between Jesus and the woman:

> But the woman, knowing what had been done to her, came in fear and trembling and fell down before him, and told him the whole truth. And he said to her, 'Daughter, your faith has made you well; go in peace, and be healed of your disease.' (vv. 33 f.)

With this scene, what looked like a superstitious act is transformed into a personal encounter. The woman falls down at Jesus' feet in the attitude of petitionary prayer. Jesus addresses her personally, 'daughter', and praises her faith. Like the friends of the paralytic digging through the roof, like blind Bartimaeus flinging away his garment, the woman, by touching Jesus' garment, attests her faith, her 'energetic grasping' for the help of God. Nor is she just 'made well' (RSV). She is made *whole*; she becomes a partaker in that wholeness of life which is the Messianic salvation. There is one unsatisfactory feature to the story; the personal encounter happens only after the healing. It should, as Matthew saw (Matt. 9.22), have been the other way round.

The raising of the girl is likewise transformed. Jesus tells the crowd, 'The child is not dead, but sleeping.' Most languages, of course, use sleep as an euphemism for death, but here sleep and death are contrasted. When we sleep we expect to get up again in the morning, but death is final. So from God's point of view, the girl is sleeping; she will rise again. Death is now not final. Again, by telling his readers the meaning of *Talitha cumi*, the narrator shows that it was not meant just as a magic formula, and in translating it he inserts the phrase 'I say to you', which is always a claim to Messianic authority. Thus the narrator is at pains to insist that the raising of the girl is the act of God. Here is the long-awaited Messianic intervention; the dead are raised.

There can be little doubt that *the feedings of the five thousand* (6.30-44) *and of the four thousand* (8.1-10) are different versions of the same incident. The statistics and minor details vary, but these are just the features which are likely to get altered in oral transmission. The basic facts are the same. Both versions have the form and style of a popular tale. The initial dialogue between Jesus and his disciples underlines the helplessness of the disciples and the wonder-worker's mastery of the situation. The actual occurrence of the miracle is veiled, as in the marriage at Cana, being merely hinted at in the gathering of the leavings and in the climacteric statement of the number fed. All this is in popular style. Are there any distinctively Christian features? At first sight, it looks as though the language describing the blessing and distribution of the bread and fish is deliberately designed to recall the Christian eucharist. The fourth gospel has clearly interpreted the miracle in this way, and there are features in Matthew's accounts which suggest the same line of interpretation. But we cannot be sure that this interpretation has already coloured the oral tradition, for the actions of Jesus are the actions of any devout Jew presiding at a meal.

There are, however, two features in the two Marcan accounts which point to an Old Testament background. They are both located in a desert. This recalls the manna story in Exodus (16.4 ff.). Both conclude with the remark, 'the people ate and were satisfied'. When they ate the manna in the desert, the children of Israel likewise ate and were satisfied (Ps. 105.40; cf. Ps. 81.16). When Israel was faithful she continued to eat and be satisfied in the land of Canaan (Deut. 14.29). When she was rebellious she was not satisfied (Lev. 26.26; Ps. 81.16; Isa. 9.20; Micah 6.14). So the prophets and psalmists looked forward to the day when once more God's people would eat and be satisfied (Jer. 31.14; Ps. 22.26). Thus the feeding of the multitude by Jesus looks back to miraculous feeding of Israel in the wilderness, and forward to the 'great feast in the Messianic age, when all should be filled and when the meek should eat and be satisfied' (Hoskyns).

Another possible interpretation of the feeding of the multitude should be noted. Some have connected it with Elisha's miraculous feeding (II Kings 4.42 ff.). 'Give to the men that they may eat' (v. 43) has been compared with 'give it them to eat' in Mark 6.37. A hundred men are fed with twenty loaves, and there was 'some' left over. It is difficult to resist the impression that the Elisha story has had some influence over the way the feeding of the multitude is told. It may even account for the origin of the story. But the background of Exodus manna and Messianic feast, which undoubtedly is also present in the text, provides a stronger theological interpretation.

The walking on the water (6.45-52) represents, as we have already suggested, a combination of two motifs: the stilling of the storm, and the appearance of Jesus on the water, which has been superimposed upon it. The reason for this combination is the desire to give a theological meaning to a popular miracle story. The transformed version has the features of a divine revelation, for the words 'He meant to pass by them', indicate the mysterious behaviour of a divine Being (cf. Exod. 34.6; I Kings 19.11). Note also the terror of the disciples, who thought it was an apparition; the reassurance, 'Take heart . . . have no fear'; and finally the word of self-manifestation, 'I AM' (RSV: 'it is I'). Here is revelation of the Old Testament God in the person of Jesus. But what of the walking on the water? In the Old Testament Yahweh also walks on the water:

> Thy way was through the sea,
> thy path through the great waters;
> Yet thy footprints were unseen (Ps. 77.19).
> Who alone . . . trampled the waves of the sea
> (Job 9.8).
> Have you [Yahweh has!] entered into the spring of the sea,
> or walked in the recesses of the deep?
> (Job 38.16).

The sea in the Old Testament stands for the uncanny power of chaos and death which threatens God's kingly rule. The theological point of this story is that in Jesus God is asserting his sovereignty over the uncanny realm of Satan. Although this story has been constructed by the early church, it not only expresses its own faith in Jesus as Messiah, but in the last resort echoes the proclamation of Jesus: 'The Reign of God has drawn nigh.'

The Syro-Phoenician woman (7.24-30) is a parallel to the Q story of the centurion (see above). Not only do the two stories possess common features; they both make the same theological point. It is through faith that the barrier between Jew and gentile is overcome, and the gentiles are admitted to the people of God. In the case of the Syro-Phoenician woman's daughter this thought is conveyed in the dialogue.

> JESUS: Let the children first be fed, for it is not right to take the children's bread and throw it to the dogs.
>
> WOMAN: Yes, Lord; yet even the dogs under the table eat the children's crumbs.

Jesus is the giver of the Messianic bread. This bread was intended 'first' (so even Paul, Rom. 1.16) for the children (of Israel): but the dogs (i.e. the gentiles) may participate in the Messianic salvation, although this privilege comes through faith alone. We can see the early church wrestling here with the problem of the gentile mission.

The deaf mute (7.32-37) and *the blind man at Bethsaida* (8.22-26) are, it will be recalled, the two healings which come closest to popular miracle tales. Neither contains any dialogue to give it theological significance. Yet there is a difference between the two narratives. The deaf mute contains a striking echo of the Old Testament, in the rare Greek word for 'had an impediment in his speech'. This word occurs elsewhere in the Greek Bible only at Isa. 35.6, where it represents the Hebrew word translated in AV and RSV as 'dumb'. Moreover, the final acclamation of the crowd has a strong Old Testament ring:

> He has done all things well;
> he even makes the deaf hear
> and the dumb speak (Mark 7.37).

We are reminded of the creation story in which God, having made everything, saw that it was good (Gen. 1.31). The healing of the deaf mute is, after all, a Messianic act, a fulfilment of Old Testament prophecy and the restoration of the goodness of the original creation.

The blind man of Bethsaida contains no dialogue or saying of Jesus, nor has it any Old Testament allusions like the deaf mute. It is a popular story, such as might be told of any wonder-worker. Possibly it is intended as a fulfilment of Isa. 35.5 ('Then shall the eyes of the blind be opened'), but the text itself does not call attention to this passage.

Sir Edwyn Hoskyns has suggested that the physical means of cure adopted in these stories may have more significance than the contemporary parallels suggest: 'Is not this contact the effective representation of the true Messianic salvation which is the lifting up of men through contact with the Messiah?'[1] This is an interesting suggestion, but it lacks a specific basis in the texts.

The epileptic boy (9.14-29) is, as we have seen, probably a combination of two different stories. The one which revolves round the contrast between Jesus and his disciples is popular in character. The other story, in which the reader's interest is focused upon the father of the boy, also has popular features: the description of the illness, the exorcism by a word of command and convulsive struggle of the demon before his final expulsion. But it is transformed by the insertion of a dialogue between the father and Jesus:

FATHER: If you can, have pity on us and help us!
JESUS: 'If you can!' All things are possible to him who believes.
FATHER: I believe; help my unbelief!

Here faith means, not belief in the power of a

[1] *Cambridge Sermons*, p. 172.

wonder-worker, but the 'energetic grasping' which can call forth an act of God. 'All things are possible to faith' is complemented by another saying in the tradition, 'All things are possible with God' (Mark 10.27). Faith on one side and the act of God on the other are between them able to do all things, even overcome the power of evil. This story probes more deeply into faith: ' "I believe; help my unbelief." Faith, that energetic grasping for the help of God, is something of which man, in his extremity, is in himself incapable. He is forced to fling himself on God's mercy. "I believe" : here the petitioner has indeed exceeded his own ability, and confesses a faith greater than he really has. "Help my unbelief" : here he who falls short of faith throws himself on the power and help of Jesus. In this paradox of faith and unbelief, as the story points out, faith becomes true and capable of receiving the miracle of God.'[1] Thus the story is transformed from a miracle tale into an illustration of faith. And in the process it is shown to be not an act of a human wonder-worker, but an act of God himself, a miracle in the biblical sense of the word.

In the healing of *blind Bartimaeus* (10.46-52), the setting, the description of the cure and, in the last sentence of v. 52, the demonstration of the cure, are all conventional. But with a few touches at each point, the story is transformed into a theologically edifying narrative. After the healing, Jesus pronounces the now familiar words, 'your faith has made you whole'. Thus, with a stroke the cure is transformed into an act of God, and Bartimaeus' persistent cry for help, his dramatic gesture in flinging off his mantle become, not the vivid traits of oriental anecdote, but a demonstration

[1] G. Bornkamm, *Jesus of Nazareth*, p. 131.

of biblical faith, his energetic, urgent grasping for the act of God. And the twice repeated cry, 'Son of David have mercy on me!' makes it a Messianic miracle. Why Son of David? Because the Messianic prophecies in Isaiah tell of the blessings that will follow when the Davidic king is restored to Israel. (Isa. 11.1 f.; linked with 35.5; 61.1 ff.). Finally Bartimaeus 'follows' Jesus 'in the way'. He becomes a disciple. The story illustrates three themes of Christian preaching: faith, Messianic salvation and discipleship.

Whatever the origins of *the cursing of the fig-tree* (11.12-14, 20-25), Mark and the oral tradition before him clearly regard it as real incident. To understand its meaning in the oral tradition, we must disregard the cleansing of the temple, which Mark has inserted into it.[1] But by stringing on to the cursing the saying in vv. 22 f. the narrator has tried to use the cursing as an illustration of the power of faith. It cannot be said that the attempt to transform this curious, and to us rather repulsive, story is successful, for the cursing of a fig-tree is hardly the sort of thing that faith ought to want to do! Hence, as we shall see, Mark has given it a symbolic meaning.

Special Lucan Material

As we have already indicated, we incline to the view that *the miraculous draft of fishes* (Luke 5.1-11) is a post-resurrection appearance which Luke has inserted at this point to illustrate the Marcan saying, 'I will make you fishers of men'. If it was a resurrection appearance in the pre-Lucan tradition, it does not call for treatment here.

[1] In the oral tradition, vv. 20 f. would have followed immediately upon v. 14.

The widow's son at Nain (7.11-17) has a number of popular features. Apollonius of Tyana tells a similar story of a raising which allegedly took place at the gates of the city of Rome. In each case the wonder-worker meets the bier and halts the funeral procession. A unique feature of this story among the synoptic miracles, but common in pagan miracle stories, is that Jesus performs the healing unbidden. There is nothing about the prayer or faith of the mother or the dead man's friends. Clearly, it was originally a popular tale. But, like the miracle stories in the Marcan tradition, especially the deaf mute, it has been Christianized by a number of traits deliberately chosen to recall the raisings performed by Elijah (I Kings 17.17 ff.; II Kings 4.18 ff.). The incident is located at Nain, quite close to Shunem, where Elisha's raising took place. The mother of the dead man is a widow, as in the Elijah story. The concluding words, 'He gave him to his mother' are identical in both stories. And at the end the crowd hails Jesus as a great prophet, the Messianic prophet like Elijah.

The story of *the bent woman* (13.10-17) contains a number of conventional traits. The length of the illness is stated and the symptoms described. The healing is accomplished by a word and a manual technique. The success of the cure is demonstrated by the acclamation of the crowd. But between the healing and the acclamation[1] there is inserted a dialogue about the sabbath, reminiscent of the withered hand and the dropsical man. The theological point (healing on the sabbath as a sign of the sabbath's fulfilment in the Messianic redemp-

[1] This is unusual: generally the dialogue comes between the diagnosis and the cure.

tion) is the same as in the story of the withered hand. But the point is brought out in a new way. The ruler of the synagogue protests: 'There are six days on which work ought to be done; come on those days and be healed.' If it were an ordinary humanitarian act, his reasoning would be unquestionable. Jesus, however, replies: 'Ought not this woman, a daughter of Abraham whom Satan bound for eighteen years, be loosed from this bond on the sabbath day?' Here is the point: as a daughter of Abraham, a member of the chosen race to whom the promises were given, she has every right to receive the blessings of the Reign of God to which the sabbath pointed forward: she *ought* to be released from the bondage of Satan precisely on the sabbath day.

The dropsical man (14.1-6) is a clear case of an 'ideal scene' constructed to carry a saying of Jesus:

> 'Which of you having an ass [some MSS read 'son'] or an ox that has fallen into a well will not immediately pull him out on the sabbath day?' (v. 5).[1]

This saying throws light on the way the miracles were understood in the tradition. They are comparable to raising an animal out of a well (or pit). In healing men and women Jesus is rescuing them out of the supreme plight of humanity. Hoskyns (*op. cit.*, p. 171) compares the 'frequent pits and snares of evil in the Psalms' (e.g. 30.3; 31.4; 35.7; 40.2). Be that as it may, the saying clearly interprets Jesus' healings as the works of the Messianic salvation.

The last miracle in the Special Lucan tradition is *the*

[1] That this saying was originally detached is indicated by Matthew's insertion of a similar saying into Mark's story of the withered hand (Matt. 12.11).

ten lepers (17.11-19). This looks like a Samaritan preacher's adaptation of Mark's healing of the leper. At first sight the command, 'Go, show yourselves to the priests', looks out of place in this story. Why should a Samaritan, of all people, show himself to a Jewish priest? Yet it remains integral to the story, for it explains how the healing did not take place until after they had left Jesus and so only the Samaritan *returned*. But it is not a mere homily on the importance of thanksgiving. The story of Naaman the Syrian (II Kings 5.8 ff.), to which the Special Lucan material also alludes in the sermon at Nazareth, has seemingly played a part in shaping our story. Naaman, too, was a leper. He too returned and gave thanks. He too was a Syrian, an outsider, not a member of the chosen people. Thus the ten lepers is another missionary story, like the centurion of Capernaum and the Syro-Phoenician woman.

Conclusion

In summing up the meaning of the miracles in the oral tradition before the gospels were written, we cannot do better than to quote what Hoskyns wrote of the miracles in Mark:

> The Marcan miracle narratives, which at first sight seem to record conventional actions of a wonder-worker, are found upon closer investigation to have a wholly different significance. The Marcan miracles are signs that the Messiah is present in the heart of Judaism, and signs warranted by Old Testament prophecy. Moreover, they are not only signs of His presence, they are signs of the nature of His power, since they point . . . away from mere physical healing to

freedom from sin and to the recognition of the power of the Living God.[1]

What Hoskyns says of the miracles in the Marcan tradition applies with equal force to the miracles in our other primary sources, Q and Special Luke.

We must remember here that we have been speaking of the miracles as they were interpreted in the early church's preaching. They are not primarily descriptions of what Jesus actually did, although (as we saw in the previous chapter) the traditions usually rest on some sort of memory, whether general or specific. Nor does the church simply reproduce the miracles as signs of the inbreaking of the final Reign of God. Jesus did *not* interpret them as signs that he was the Messiah. The early church, however, interpreted them just in this sense—*as works of the Messiah.*

This is not a wholly new meaning, arbitrarily imposed upon the miracles. To begin with, although Jesus did not interpret his miracles Messianically in a direct or explicit way, they were for him *implicitly* Messianic: for they involved the claim that in and through him God was now beginning his saving work. Secondly, the explicit Messianic faith of the church is the result of the resurrection appearances, in which Jesus was manifested for what he really was: the one in whom God had acted for men's salvation. And lastly, to say Jesus is Messiah is not to accord him some exalted status for his own sake, apart from God: it is to say that he is the one in whom God has acted decisively for man's salvation, and the one in whom God continues so to act in the on-going life of the church.

[1] *Cambridge Sermons*, pp. 175-6.

It was to proclaim what God was continuing to do that the earliest church used the miracle stories. In the church God through Jesus Christ still does what he had done through him in Galilee. He releases men and women from the grip of evil, and gives them the blessings of his salvation.

4

INTERPRETING THE MIRACLES IN THE SYNOPTIC GOSPELS

Five Groups of Miracles in Mark

IT IS generally agreed that Mark[1] was the first gospel writer. He was the first to compose a written document consisting of a passion story, prefaced by snapshot scenes from the ministry of Jesus and collections of his sayings. Mark has been likened to a collection of beads on a string. The beads are the originally isolated units of material of various types, including the two types of miracle stories which we discussed in the previous chapter, and the string is the framework constructed by the evangelist to tie the units together. Mark has also been called a passion story with an extended preface, a description which calls attention to the fact that the originally isolated units, including the miracle stories, have been given a new meaning by their connection with the passion and resurrection of Jesus. In order to discover the meaning which the evangelist places upon the miracle of Jesus, we must study the arrangement and ordering of the miracles, the editorial modifications which Mark has made in the body of the stories, and the editorial links by which he has tied them together into a continuous narrative.

[1] The traditional names of the gospels are used without prejudging the question of authorship. All four gospels were originally anonymous writings; the titles, 'According to Matthew', etc., were added later.

Mark's *opening* miracle is the Capernaum demoniac, followed by Simon's mother-in-law and a generalized summary, the healings at eventide. This first series of miracles follows almost immediately upon the baptism and temptation (1.9-11, 12 f.) and Mark's summary of Jesus' message (1.14-15). Jesus has been endowed at his baptism with the Spirit of God, the dynamic power of God's saving action of the last days. In his temptation he has won the first round of the conflict with Satan and the powers of evil. In the power of the Spirit and in the strength of this first victory he now sallies forth to proclaim the inbreaking of God's Reign, the wresting of Satan's power from him, and to continue the struggle against the foe. It is thus no accident that Mark's first miracle is an exorcism. He introduces it with an editorial comment on Jesus' teaching with *authority* or power (1.22). This word harks back to his endowment with the Spirit at his baptism and is again underlined in the comment of the bystanders, added to the tradition by Mark himself, 'What is this? A new teaching! With authority he commands even the unclean spirits, and they obey him' (v. 27). At first sight the connection between teaching and exorcism appears artificial, but the teaching which follows (e.g. the conflict stories of 2.1-3.6) is controversial in character and, therefore, like the exorcisms, part of Jesus' conflict with his enemies. In his teaching Jesus is in conflict with his human enemies, as in the miracles he is in conflict with the demons and with sickness. Although, as we have seen, Simon's mother-in-law was originally a biographical reminiscence, for Mark it is a constitution of the conflict with the powers of evil. The healings at eventide summarize this phase of the ministry and provide the transition to the next section. It introduces the theme of the 'Messianic secret', to be discussed later.

The *second* group of miracles occurs in a series of conflicts with human enemies (Mark 1.40-3.6). This series opens with the leper and contains the paralytic and the withered hand. The story of the leper introduces the theme of the Mosaic Law, and Jesus' claim at once to fulfil and to supersede it, a claim which leads to the ensuing disputes with the 'scribes of the Pharisees'. In healing the paralytic Jesus victoriously asserts against his critics his *authority* (note the recurrence in 2.10 of this key word from Chapter 1) to remit sins. In healing the withered hand he asserts his authority to 'do good'[1] and to 'save life' on the sabbath. As Messiah he at once fulfils the law and supersedes it. The conflicts culminate in a resolution of Jesus' enemies to destroy him (3.6). As a historical note that remark would have been premature, but its intention is theological: Mark is telling us that these disputes, including those occasioned by the healings, are not isolated incidents in the life of Jesus, but part of a conflict which is to culminate with his passion. The evangelist is relating the miracles to the passion in a way which the tradition has never done before. But he is not imposing a meaning on the miracles which was alien either to the earlier tradition or to Jesus himself. For on the earlier tradition the miracles were manifestations of Jesus' Messiahship. But this was a belief to which the church had come as a result of the death and resurrection of Jesus, and therefore the very telling of these stories had always presumed faith in Jesus' death and resurrection.

[1] The Greek word for 'it is lawful' in 3.4 comes from the same root as the word 'authority'.

And for Jesus himself, the miracles had been signs of the dawning kingdom of God: they derived their meaning and significance solely from what was still to come. The church now knows that with the death and resurrection of Jesus the kingdom has in a very real sense already come.

At the close of this section, Mark has composed a generalized summary as a transition to the next section, just as 1.32-34 joins the Capernaum miracles with the conflict stories. The summary concludes with exorcisms, the *third* group of miracles, and prepares the way for the Beelzebul controversy (3.22-30). In this episode Mark spells out clearly the meaning of the exorcisms: they are the struggle between the Spirit of God and powers of evil. The strong man is being bound, prior to the plundering of his goods in the passion and resurrection. Mark surely intends his readers to recall Isa. 53.12:

> Therefore will I divide him a portion with the great,
> and he shall divide the spoil with the strong.

There is a *fourth* group of miracles in 4.35-5.43, all of them stupendous in character. They are: the stilling of the storm, the Gerasene demoniac, and the raising of Jairus' daughter—with its inset, the woman with the haemorrhage. Probably the collection had already been made before Mark, and all he has done is to add the command to secrecy, which will be discussed later (see below, p. 75 f.). How, then, does he mean us to understand these miracles? Note how he has placed them immediately after the parables of Chapter 4, in which Jesus revealed to the disciples as a privileged group the secret of the kingdom of God (4.11; cf. v. 34). Now the disciples are the only people present at the stilling of the storm. Their presence is taken for granted in the exorcism of the Gerasene demoniac. They play a prominent part (though, typically, an uncomprehending one) in the healing of the woman with the haemorrhage, while three of them—Peter, James and John—are taken in to see the raising of the girl. These miracles, following as they do hard upon the parables, are thus manifestations to the disciples of the secret of the kingdom of God. But the disciples are slow to grasp the secret. In a sense, Jesus is now in conflict with his disciples, and the conflict will not be resolved until Peter confesses at Caesarea Philippi, 'You are the Christ'.

At the end of this section one would expect a generalized summary as at 1.32-34 and 3.7-12. Instead, the rejection at Nazareth follows, with a kind of negative generalized summary: 'He could do no mighty works there, except that he laid his hands upon a few sick people and healed them. And he marvelled because of their unbelief' (6.5 f.). Only here does Mark make Jesus' healings expressly dependent upon faith, though he had implied it in the cases of the paralytic (2.5) and of the woman with the haemorrhage (5.34). They are acts of *God*, for faith always implies the act of God at the other end. Jesus is confronted with the refusal of his own countrymen to hear, to see and to understand. Once again he is engaged in conflict with the unbelief and misunderstanding of men.

In the sending forth of the twelve (6.7-13) Jesus shares his authority with his disciples. The area of the conflict widens. But with the disciples, as with their Master, the exorcisms and healings must be subordinated to the message of the coming reign of God (vv. 12 f.).

In 6.30-8.26 there is a *fifth* group of miracles, the feeding of the five thousand, the walking on the water, a generalized summary of healings, the Syro-Phoenician woman, the deaf mute, the feeding of the four thousand, and the blind man of Bethsaida. The discourse to the disciples in 8.14-21 welds this section into a unity. It deals with the meaning of the multiplying of the loaves, which the disciples are not able to perceive. This theme of loaves and the eating of bread runs like a thread all through this section. It is present in the walking on the water (6.52, an editorial addition of Mark), in the discourse on purity (7.1-23) and in the story of the Syro-Phoenician woman (7.24-30). The discourse with the disciples underlines their failure to understand all these incidents.

This section, then, continues Jesus' struggle with the disciples' misunderstanding. Mark still keeps us guessing what the mystery is, but he ends this section with the opening of the eyes of the blind man. The disciples' misunderstanding will be removed immediately afterwards with Peter's confession, the transfiguration and the teaching about the passion. The secret is that Jesus is the Christ and that he must die and rise again! The disciples' eyes are opened. Then, by placing blind Bartimaeus at the conclusion of this section, Mark again gives it a symbolic meaning which it did not have in the tradition. Bartimaeus personifies the disciples: their eyes are opened, and they follow Jesus 'in the way', going up to Jerusalem for the passion (10.52). Finally, Mark gives the cursing of the fig tree a symbolic meaning by inserting within it the cleansing of the temple. Both incidents are curtain-raisers to the passion. The cleansing of the temple symbolizes God's judgement over Judaism and its replacement by the Messianic sacrifice and temple; while the cursing of the fig-tree symbolizes God's judgement on Israel for its barrenness.

The Messianic Secret in Mark

One of the most puzzling aspects of Mark is the series of passages in which a command is given either to the demons or to the persons healed to remain silent. The demons (1.25, 34; 3.12) are enjoined to be silent about the Messiahship of Jesus, which they have supernaturally perceived. The recipients of cures (1.44; 5.43; 7.36; 8.26) are enjoined to be silent about the healing itself. Most of these passages occur in the evangelist's editorial sections, either in his generalized summaries (1.34; 3.12) or in his additions to the units of material (5.43; 7.36; 8.26). These additions create inconsistencies: either the command to silence is disobeyed (7.36), or it is given in circumstances in which it was manifestly impossible to observe (5.43). The inconsistencies show that the theme of the secret was not already present, still less a historical fact in Jesus' ministry, but a creation of the evangelist himself. Only in two places is the command to silence earlier than Mark: in 1.25 and 1.44, where it is integral to the respective stories. In 1.25 it is simply a conventional feature, portraying the struggle between the exorcist and the demons, while in 1.44 it simply reinforces the urgency of the command, 'Go and show yourself to the priest'. But in both these instances Mark doubtless means the command to secrecy in the light of his theory. The theory also appears to conflict with the tremendous success of the ministry. If Jesus sought to play down his miracles, why is it that the attempt was so unsuccessful? Of course, the amazement of the bystanders was a traditional feature at the end of the story of healing. Yet, in his own editorial sections, Mark has gone out of his way to stress the amazement of the crowds and the way they flocked to Jesus.[1] But the contradiction is more apparent than real. The crowd may be amazed, but they do not really understand (4.12; 6.15; 8.28). Nor are the disciples any better (4.13, 40; and esp. 6.52; 8.14-21) until Peter's confession (8.29). Only then does Peter, as the mouthpiece of the disciples, come to see what the demons had supernaturally perceived, that Jesus is the Messiah. But, like the demons, he is at once enjoined to silence (8.30). From this point Jesus begins to reveal to the disciples that as Messiah (Son of man) he must suffer. This, too, must be kept secret until *after the resurrection* (9.9).

Here is the clue to this elaborate theological construction. The Messianic secret is really an aside addressed to the reader. He is intended to see that the miracles, along with the other disclosures of Jesus in his ministry, are revelations of the *risen* Christ *addressed to him,* the reader. As revelations during the earthly life of Jesus they are mysterious, indirect, paradoxical in character. The theory is the consequence of Mark's combination of the isolated units of tradition with the story of the passion. It is the same problem which in Phil. 2.6-11 is solved differently by the conception of the incarnate life of Christ as a self-emptying of his glory. On that view there would be no place for miracles as open manifestations of the divine glory. The fourth gospel has thrown the paradox to the winds, yet John also, as

[1] At 1.22, 28, 32-34, 39, 45; 2.1 f., 13; 3.7-12; 4.1-2; 6. 32 f.; 9.15.

we shall see, insists on the preliminary character of the 'signs'.

Ten Miracles in Matthew

Matthew's gospel is a new edition of Mark. Parts of Mark have been rearranged and parts have been omitted; material has been added from other sources (Q and Special Matthean material), and a small amount of material specially composed by the evangelist himself.

In chapters 8-9 Matthew has grouped together into one section most of the miracles contained in three sections of Mark, the Capernaum miracles of Mark 1, the conflict stories of Mark 2-3.6, and the divine revelations of Mark 4.35-5.43. To these he has added one miracle from Q and closed the section with two compositions of his own. The result is a collection of ten miracles:

1. The leper (Mark), 8.1-4.
2. The centurion (Q), 8.5-13.
3. Simon's mother-in-law (Mark), 8.14 f.

Here follows a Marcan summary, the healings at eventide, with an added quotation from Isa. 53.4, then some Q sayings about discipleship (8.18-22).

4. The stilling of the storm (Mark) 8.23-27.
5. The Gadarene demoniacs (Mark) 8.28-34.
6. The paralytic (Mark), 9.1-8.

Here follow two conflict stories which are not miracles, as in Mark 2.

7, 8. The synagogue ruler's daughter and the woman with the haemorrhage (Mark), 9.18-26.

9. Two blind men (based on Mark 8.22-26 and 10.46-52), 9.27-31.

10. The dumb demoniac (based on Mark's deaf-mute), 9.32-34.

The collection closes with a summary statement (9.35) of Jesus' teaching, preaching, and healing, which is almost identical in wording with 4.23, thus linking Chapters 8-9 with the sermon on the mount (Chapters 5-7).

Matthew has composed these chapters with great care. He brings these miracles together in this way not because he thinks that Mark had got them in the wrong order, nor simply because he wants to tidy up the narrative. Matthew's purpose is theological, or, more properly, Christological. The miracles are 'the works of the Messiah' (11.2), just as the sermon on the mount is the teaching of the Messiah. As Messiah, Jesus is the second Moses. He delivers the new law on the mount (Chapters 5-7) as Moses delivered the law on Mount Sinai, and then performs ten miracles as Moses brought about the ten plagues (Exod. 7-11). Note, too, how the healing of the leper culminates in the command that he should show himself to the priest 'and offer the gift that Moses commanded, for a proof to the people'. Matthew deliberately omits *what* the leper did (Mark 1.45), so the command itself becomes the climax in which Jesus declares himself to be the fulfilment of Moses.[1] Again, after the first three miracles and the generalized summary, Matthew typically adds an Old Testament quotation: 'This was to fulfil what was spoken by the prophet Isaiah, "He took our infirmities and bore our diseases" '

[1] Cf. above pp. 49 f. Matthew does not innovate: his interpretation of the miracles only serves to bring out more clearly what was already in the tradition.

(8.17). The miracles are works of the servant of Yahweh. In the Old Testament Moses was supremely the servant of Yahweh and the servant prophecies foretell, in Matthew's view, the works of the second Moses, who triumphantly leads men[1] from the bondage of infirmity and disease as Moses led Israel from the bondage of Pharaoh. The point is clinched by another servant quotation from Isaiah which occurs in Matthew's second group of miracles (withered hand followed by generalized summary, Beelzebul controversy and the demand for a sign) in 12.18-21. This comes from Isa. 42.1-4, and concludes with a significant and deliberate alteration of the Hebrew text: 'till he brings justice to victory' (v. 20). The miracles of Jesus are again the triumphant deeds of the second Moses, the servant of Yahweh. The Beelzebul controversy which follows continues this interpretation.

Matthew's third group of miracles (14.13-15.39) is taken from the group in Mark 6-8:

The feeding of the five thousand, 14.13-21.
The walking on the water, 14.22-33, followed by a generalizing summary, vv. 34-6.
The Canaanitish woman, 15.21-28.
A generalized summary replacing the deaf-mute, 15.29-31.
The feeding of the four thousand, 15.32-39.

In Mark the dominant theme of this section was the conflict between Jesus and the disciples' misunderstanding, a conflict which prepared the way for Peter's con-

[1] 'Took' and 'bore' in this quotation do not mean that Jesus himself endured the sicknesses and diseases—there is no trace of such an idea in Matthew—but that he *triumphantly* took them away.

fession of faith. Matthew drops this theme.[1] But the disciples are still in the centre of the picture. Their active role in the feedings is more strongly emphasized (note the careful rewording of the introductory dialogues between Jesus and the disciples), as is the connection of these meals with the eucharist (note the almost complete disappearance of the fish as a separate course, reflecting the Christian 'breaking of the bread'). In the feedings Jesus acts as the Lord of his church, continuing his ministry through his disciples.

The alterations to the walking on the water are even more striking. Though still a revelation, it is no longer a revelation which produces perplexity. First, Peter (who is to be instituted as primate of the Twelve in 16.18) walks on the water like his Lord—he preeminently will continue the Lord's work after the ascension. But Jesus, the Lord, continues his ministry in earthen vessels: in his littleness of faith Peter falls, and is in danger of sinking. He cries out to be saved from the waters (14.30), as the psalmist had cried out to Yahweh (Ps. 69.1). No wonder, when the Lord rescues Peter, the disciples worship him and confess: 'Truly you are the Son of God.'

The dialogue between Jesus and the Canaanitish woman is expanded to bring out the point that it is faith which overcomes the barrier between Jew and Gentile. Jesus decides a crucial issue that vexed the Jewish-Christian church. Thus this whole group of miracles portrays Jesus as the Lord of his church, empowering and authorizing his disciples to follow him and to be the ministerial agents of his continuing ministry.

[1] Note the omission of Mark 6.52 at Matt. 14.33, and the alteration to Mark 8.14-21 in 16.5-12.

It is instructive to watch Matthew handling the individual miracles. On the one hand he abbreviates them considerably. Thus the exorcism of the Gadarene demoniacs is reduced from twenty verses in Mark to seven in Matthew, and the epileptic boy from sixteen verses to eight. But it is important to notice which features Matthew reduces. It is always the features where Mark is closest to the oral tradition, the conventional traits of the popular miracle story. These Matthew reduces to a brief, stereotyped formula: 'And behold, a leper came to him and knelt before him saying . . .' (Matt. 8.2) and the similar formulae at 8.5; 9.18, 20, 28; 15.22; 17.14.

Never does Matthew reduce the dialogue: in fact he sometimes expands it. In the treatment of these dialogues, Matthew is concerned pre-eminently with two themes, faith and discipleship. Note especially the prominence of such phrases as 'your faith has made you well' (9.22); 'According to your faith be it done to you' (9.29); 'be it done for you as you have believed' (8.13; cf. 15.28); 'Do you believe that I am able to do this?' (9.28). The omission of 'your faith has made you well' from the blind man of Jericho (Matt. 20.34; contrast Mark 10.52) is best explained from the fact that Matthew treats this story under his other theme, that of discipleship. In connection with discipleship, we remember the group of miracles in Chapters 14-15 already discussed, and we note also the epileptic boy, in which the theme of the father is dropped and the emphasis shifted exclusively to the disciples' inability to cure the boy. The stilling of the storm (8.23-27), which in Mark was an epiphany scene, is transformed by Matthew into an illustration of discipleship by the insertion of the two pronouncements on discipleship from Q immediately before it (vv. 18-22) and of the introductory link 'his disciples *followed* him' (v. 23).

Matthew, then, is not just a collector and preserver of the miracle tradition. He expounds that tradition in a way which is relevant to the needs of the church in his day. Like Mark, he is not just telling stories of things that happened in the past, but proclaiming Jesus Christ as the Lord of his continuing church. Yet he is not an innovator, but an expositor of a tradition he has received. Behind that exposition lies the conviction that the same Jesus who lived and worked in Galilee is the one who said 'Lo, I am with you always, to the close of the age.

The Meaning of Miracles to Luke

Like Matthew, Luke is a product of the sub-apostolic age, and although he never uses the word church in his gospel he, too, has a strong 'church-consciousness'. Indeed, he follows his gospel with the Acts of the Apostles; his total work is a history of the Christian church in two volumes. The gospel is part I of that history, dealing with what Jesus 'began to do and to teach'. It is essentially a 'narrative' (Luke 1.1), and is in fact the first life of Jesus. Mark had presented the story of Jesus as the final conflict with the powers of evil. For Matthew, Christ was the second Moses, the founder legislator and teacher of the new Israel, who will judge its life by his own standards when he comes again. Luke is concerned primarily with the *deeds* of Jesus; his teaching is secondary (Luke 24.19; Acts 1.1).

Luke's over-all plan is succinctly stated at 13.32: 'Behold, I cast out demons and perform cures today and tomorrow, and the third day I finish my course.' Jesus' ministry is divided into three phases. The first 'day', part I, is the Galilean ministry (Luke 4.14-9.50); part II, the second 'day', is the journey to Jerusalem (9.51-18.34); and the third 'day' is the passion at Jerusalem (18.35-end). Parts I and II are marked by miracles ('cast out demons and perform cures'); there are no miracles in part III.[1] Indeed the miracles are the chief features of parts I and II, although there are only three miracles, (the bent woman, the dropsical man and the ten lepers) in part II.

Part I opens with the sermon in the synagogue at Nazareth, which Luke has deliberately moved from its Marcan position (Mark 6.1-6) and placed here as a frontispiece to the ministry. The text is from Isa. 61.1-2:

> The Spirit of the Lord is upon me,
> because he has anointed me to preach good news to the poor.
> He has sent me to proclaim release to the captives
> and recovering of sight to the blind,
> to set at liberty those who are oppressed,
> to proclaim the acceptable year of the Lord.

Then follows the exposition: '*Today* this scripture has been fulfilled in your hearing' (4.21). 'Today' covers the ministry of Jesus inaugurated by his endowment with the Spirit at his baptism. This is the period of the fulfilment of the Old Testament prophecy, the age when the salvation of God is present in the world. Jesus is laying down the programme for his coming ministry. This is made clear in the curious v. 23, 'Doubtless you will quote me this proverb, "Physician, heal yourself;

[1] The sole exception is the healing of the high priest's servant's ear, 22.51, a typical touch of Lucan pathos.

what we have heard you did at Capernaum, do here also in your own country".' There are no miracles at Capernaum until 4.31 ff., and it looks at first sight like a blunder—as though Luke has forgotten that he has shifted the scene to the beginning of the ministry. Note, however, the future tense: 'You *will* say.' Jesus is talking of what *will be* the reaction of the people of Nazareth when he has carried out his programme. That reaction actually occurs at 8.19-21; Jesus' mother and brothers come to 'see' him, i.e. to see his miracles as Herod also wished (9.9). Confronted by Jesus' healings, the people of Nazareth will react like the widows and lepers in the days of Elijah and Elisha. Rejected by their own people, the two Old Testament prophets had turned instead to outsiders—the widow of Sarepta and Naaman the Syrian. So Jesus, rejected by his own people, would turn to the outcast—to women, Samaritans and gentiles.

Luke deliberately postpones the call of Simon until after the Capernaum miracles; Jesus begins at once to execute the programme of his sermon.

The call of Simon is preceded by the miraculous draught of fishes. Simon had also presumably witnessed the cure of his mother-in-law. Thus it is as a worker of miracles that Jesus calls his disciples, not just by his word, as in Mark. This shows again how for Luke the miracles are the most important aspect of Jesus' ministry.

Next comes the group of conflict stories from Mark, containing the leper, the paralytic and the withered hand (Luke 5.12-6.11). Whereas Matthew abbreviates the narrative part of the miracles and throws the dialogue between Jesus and the patient into sharper relief, Luke keeps the narrative part in full and actually improves on Mark's style. He often enhances the seriousness of the illness. Unlike Matthew, who tones it down, he accentuates the popular notion of Jesus' power to heal as a kind of magic. He emphasizes the suddenness of the cure, and the amazement of the crowds. In these ways he reverses the trend, noticeable in Matthew as compared with Mark, away from the popular miracle story.[1] Yet it would be wrong to see in Luke merely a popular story-teller who thinks of Jesus merely as a wonder-worker. Luke places his art at the service of his theology. His interest is always in the deeds of Jesus as a fulfilment of prophecy. This is stressed in the sermon of Nazareth, and it is repeated in the answer to John (7.20-22). Note how Luke has prefixed to the answer to John the raising of the widow's son at Nain (7.11-17) and has inserted into Q the summary statement of v. 21. The healings, exorcisms and raising from the dead are

[1] Examples: Matthew has cut out the opening scene from the paralytic; Luke retains it and improves on Mark's style. He describes more photographically the scene of Jesus and the woman with the haemorrhage (8.47). Whereas Matthew had abbreviated the description of the epileptic boy's disease, Luke elaborates it (9.39), and draws more sharply the contrast between the apprentices and the wonder-worker. In the story of the blind man of Jericho the scene is pictured more clearly: Luke explains how the blind man knew it was *Jesus* approaching (18.37), and how he found his way to Jesus despite his blindness (v. 40: Jesus commands others to bring him).

The seriousness of the illness is enhanced at 5.12 ('full of leprosy') and at 9.39. The suddenness of the cure is emphasized at 5.25; 8.44, 47, 55, and the amazement of the crowds at 5.26; 7.16; 18.43. For healing as a kind of magic cf. 5.17: 'The power of the Lord was with him to heal.'

Other popular traits are the giving of a name to the previously anonymous (see above, 35, n.) ruler of the synagogue (Jairus, 8.41), and the touch of pathos in the statement that his daughter, like the widow's son at Nain (7.12), was an only child (8.42).

all signs that Jesus is the prophet-Messiah sent from God: in him the salvation of God is present in history. Moreover, the final acclamations of the crowd are given a typically biblical twist. Their praises are addressed not to the wonder-worker but to *God* (5.26; 7.16; 18.43).

Luke's 'great omission' of Mark 6.45-8.26 has long puzzled scholars. The reasons for it need not concern us here, but it does result in the omission of the walking on the water, the summary of the healings at Gennesaret, the Syro-Phoenician woman, the deaf-mute, the second feeding, the discourse on the two feedings and the blind man of Bethsaida. The effect is that the central crisis is no longer, as in Mark, associated with the blindness of the disciples. Instead, the feeding of the five thousand, Peter's confession, and the transfiguration follow in quick succession, all of them being (vaguely) located at Bethsaida. The feeding is no longer an unexplained riddle, but a clearly understood revelation.

Both missionary charges, to the twelve and to the seventy, include the command to heal (9.1; 10.9). This foreshadows the place of healing in the apostolic church, as depicted later in Acts. The miracles are not only events in the life of Jesus. They are examples of what Jesus will continue to do through his apostles after he is taken up. But there must be a right attitude to the miracles on the part of the Christian ministry: 'Nevertheless, do not rejoice in this, that the spirits are subject to you; but rejoice that your names are written in heaven' (10.20). Whereas the miracles were the central feature of Jesus' mission, for the apostles they will be incidental corroborations of their mission. And they must not rejoice in them, but only in their own election.

Finally, Luke fully recognizes the double-edged

character of the miracles. They are never conclusive proofs of Jesus' Messiahship. A curiosity which seeks to 'see' the miracles of Jesus, as Herod did (9.9 ff.) cannot be gratified. Signs can never be granted on request. The only sign is the sign of the prophet Jonah, his preaching of repentance (11.29 ff.). Of course it is possible to see the true meaning of the miracles: if Tyre and Sidon had seen them they would have repented long ago (10.13-16). Yet Chorazin, Bethsaida and Capernaum saw them and did not repent. Miracles are proofs of Jesus' mission, but not conclusive proofs. Nowhere is this so clearly expressed as in the parable of the rich man and Lazarus (16.19-31). It is no good sending back Lazarus to warn the surviving brothers of the rich man; if they won't listen to the testimony of scripture, they won't be persuaded even by such a stupendous miracle as a resurrection. Miracle is a double-edged instrument. This has already been recognized in the temptation and implied in the sermon at Nazareth.

To conclude, Luke is more interested than the other evangelists in the miracles as facts of past history. They are part, and indeed the most important part, of Jesus' biography prior to his passion. Yet Luke is not uninterested in their meaning. They are characteristic of the central phase of the mighty acts of man's redemption. The Old Testament had prophesied them; they occur in Jesus; and the later church, from its own standpoint, looks back upon them, and draws lessons for the understanding of its own mission.

5

THE JOHANNINE SIGNS

The Book of Signs

THE FOURTH gospel is a restatement of the early Christian message in terms designed to make it intelligible to the Hellenistic world. This restatement is achieved by combining traditional narrative material with dialogues and discourses mainly of the evangelist's own composition.

Much of the traditional narrative material, including the miracles, seems to have come from a 'Book of Signs', a collection of miracles attributed to Jesus. The grounds for this theory are as follows: Although in 2.11 and 4.54 the marriage at Cana and the healing of the official's son are reckoned as the first and second signs of Jesus respectively, more miracles are inserted between the first and second signs (2.23; 3.2). The enumeration can be explained if it came from the Book of Signs and the evangelist has dislocated it in inserting 2.23 and 3.2. Again, 12.37 f. looks like the conclusion of the Book of Signs. As it now stands it does not properly describe the whole of Jesus' preceding ministry as presented by the evangelist, for this had included discourses as well as signs. Finally, another excerpt from the conclusion of the Book of Signs appears in 20.30, which contains a direct allusion to the Book itself.

Whether the evangelist used all the signs contained

in the Book we do not know, but at all events he has reproduced from this source seven miracles:

The marriage at Cana (2.1-11).
The official's son (4.46-54).
The lame man at Bethesda (5.1-9).
The feeding of the five thousand (6.1-13).
The walking on the water (6.16-21).
The man born blind (9.1-34).
The raising of Lazarus (11.1-44).

There are other references from the Book of Signs at 6.2 (cf. Matt. 14.14; Luke 9.11); 7.3; 11.47.

It is not always easy to distinguish between what comes from the Book of Signs and what the evangelist has added or altered. Many would think it a hopeless task. But the evangelist has a distinctive style and religious vocabulary of his own, and this often enables us to distinguish between the tradition and the editing with tolerable certainty. The following are probable additions by the evangelist:

The marriage at Cana: 2.6 (allusion to Jewish rites of purification).

The official's son: 4.46 (cross-reference to Cana); 4.48.

The lame man at Bethesda: 5.17, 18b, 19-47.

The feeding of the five thousand: 6.4 (allusion to 'feast of the Jews') 14 (qualification of prophet as the one who was to come into the 'world'), 26-65.

The man born blind: 9.3b-5, 16b, 22 f., 29-34 (excluding 'and they cast him out'), 35-37.

The raising of Lazarus: 11.4, 7-10, 16, 20-7, 40, 41b-42.

In style and form the miracle stories in the evangelist's source are similar to the miracle stories in the oral tradition behind the synoptic gospels. But the miraculous is heightened. At the marriage of Cana a colossal amount of water is involved, the equivalent of one hundred gallons (2.6). Like its Q parallel the centurion's boy, the official's son is a healing at a distance, but at a greater distance, for in the Q story Jesus is outside Capernaum where the boy is resident, while in John he is at Cana, not far short of twenty miles distant (4.46). The lame man of Bethesda had been infirm for 38 years (5.5). The feeding of the five thousand is not occasioned by any apparent need; nothing is said about the isolation of the site or of the long time the crowd had been away from home. Bread worth two hundred silver pieces (*denarii*) would *not* be enough to feed them, yet *they ate as much as they would.* In the walking on the water only traces of its earliest form, the stilling of the storm, survive, while a miraculous landing, a common feature in the pagan parallels, has been added. The blind man was *born* blind (9.1). Lazarus had been dead for four days and corruption had already set in (11.39); in Mark Jairus' daughter had only just died, while in Luke's story of the widow's son at Nain Jesus met the funeral procession on its way to the burial.

The Book of Signs seems to have been compiled at a later stage of development than the synoptic tradition. Can we venture any further suggestion as to the alternate origin of the Johannine signs? The form critics have suggested that the marriage of Cana is a transplantation from the Dionysus legend. Dionysus was the god of wine, and on his feast day, January 6, in the temples dedicated to him, water was miraculously changed into wine. The later church, it is alleged, was still aware of the connection when it appointed January

6 for the feast of the Epiphany and commemorated the marriage of Cana on that day. Professor Richardson,[1] offers a different explanation: it is a *midrash* or edifying tale spun out to correct misunderstanding of the saying, 'No one after drinking old wine desires new, for he says "The old is good"' (Luke 5.39). These theories are not mutually exclusive, but in the nature of the case they cannot be proven. All we can say for certain is that the story came into the tradition before John, probably at a later stage, and certainly along a different line of transmission from the synoptic tradition. John himself, of course, assumes that it was an actual incident in Jesus' ministry.

The official's son, as we have already noted, is a variant of the Q story of the Centurion's boy. The lame man at Bethesda is probably a variant of the paralytic (compare John 5.11 with Mark 2.9). The feeding and the walking on the water are obviously variants of their synoptic parallels, the man born blind is a variant of the cures of the blind in the synoptists (cf. Mark 8.22-26; 10.46-52).

Many critics have supposed that John has taken these stories direct from Mark, but the trend today is against this view.[2]

The raising of Lazarus is quite unknown in the synoptic tradition. If it really happened, it would present an acute problem. It would be hard to explain why the synoptists omitted it, especially since, according to John, it was the immediate cause of Jesus' arrest. This, and not any anti-miraculous prejudice, has led to such

[1] *The Miracle Stories of the Gospels* (London, 1941), p. 121.

[2] See *St John and the Synoptic Gospels*, by P. Gardner-Smith (Cambridge, 1938).

suggestions as that of Professor Richardson[1] that this is another *midrash*, on the saying in the parable of the rich man and Lazarus, 'If someone goes to them from the dead, they will repent' (Luke 16.30), a saying which has been expanded into an actual raising of Lazarus. Mary and Martha will then have come from the same cycle of tradition (Luke 10.38-42). In this case there is no need to suppose that the Book of Signs has directly borrowed from St Luke's gospel, for it may have come from the pre-Lucan source. But all we can be sure of is that this story must have come into the tradition at a stage later than, and independently of, the synoptists, and that again John takes for granted that it really happened.

How did the Book of Signs interpret the miracles? They are full of features which are common in pagan wonder stories to an even greater degree than the synoptic miracles. The two features which distinguish the synoptic stories from the pagan parallels—the specific Christian teaching in the dialogue and the colouring of the narrative with Old Testament motifs—are much less conspicuous in the Johannine signs. This gives them a much more secular character, and makes Jesus much more like a pagan wonder-worker. What distinctive Christian element there is to be seen is the use of these stories in Christian proclamation. The divine power present in Jesus is the power of the biblical God.

In the marriage at Cana Jesus' initial refusal to perform a miracle for Mary (2.4) is a typical trait. Human beings cannot command the divine power. They must wait for the wonder-worker to decide when to use it

[1] *Op. cit.*, p. 120.

As in the feeding of the multitude, the miracle itself is not described: the divine action remains a mystery, only indicated by its effects. The point of the story lies in the steward's remark: 'Every man serves the good wine first; when men have drunk freely, then the poor wine; but you have kept the good wine until now' (2.10). Here is the Christian message: the good wine has come in Jesus.[1]

In the Book of Signs the official's son, like the Centurion's boy in Q, was a missionary story. It culminates in the conversion of the official and his family: 'He himself believed, and all his household' (4.53).[2] 'Belief' in this passage means, not that 'urgent, energetic grasping' for the help of God, but accepting the gospel and becoming a Christian. And as in the stories of the Capernaum centurion and the Syro-Phoenician woman the healing at a distance, a conventional trait in itself, is pressed into the service of the missionary theme. The gentiles are admitted to salvation not by Jesus himself in his earthly ministry, but through his apostles after the resurrection.

The Bethesda[3] healing, like some of the synoptic healings, leads into a controversial dialogue (5.10-18), about the breach of the sabbath, and culminates in the resolve of Jesus' enemies to put him to death (v. 18).[4] There is less pagan influence here, and it reflects a

[1] For the association of new wine with the Kingdom of God, see Mark 14.25.

[2] For the typical missionary language, compare Acts 16.31-34.

[3] RSV reads 'Bethzatha', but in an interesting monograph on the rediscovery of the pool in Jerusalem Prof. Jeremias has shown that Bethesda (AV, NEB) is correct.

[4] Vv. 17 and 18b, which introduce the theme of the relation of the Father and the Son, come from the evangelist, and prepare the way for his expanded dialogue (vv. 19-47).

central concern of the early church—the conflict with Judaism over sabbath observance.

As in the synoptic variants, the feeding and the walking on the water are divine revelations. But they are revelations not of a pagan deity, but of the Old Testament God. As the giver of the miraculous food Jesus is hailed by the crowd as the 'Prophet' (6.14);[1] not just any prophet, but the Prophet-Messiah, who is imparting a foretaste of the Messianic banquet. Thus the final acclamation of the crowd brings out a theme already implied in the pre-Marcan tradition (see above, p. 58). The walking on the water has the same revelatory formula as in Mark: 'It is I, do not be afraid.' In Jesus the Old Testament God is revealed in action.

The Siloam healing is similar to the lame man of Bethesda, both in form and meaning. It leads into a dialogue between the cured man and Jesus' enemies.[2] The Pharisees' examination of the patient establishes the reality of the cure and leads to the charge against Jesus for the breach of the sabbath (cf. the blind man of Bethesda). The trial scene is particularly vivid. Some have attributed this to an eyewitness, others to the evangelist's own knowledge of Jewish judicial procedure. More likely it is due to the *narrator's* (not the evangelist's) first-hand acquaintance with that procedure. Jewish Christians must have frequently experienced it. The healing is also interested in the con-

[1] This is not John's own Christology. It must therefore come from the Book of Signs. The evangelist probably added: 'who is to come into the world', a typically Johannine phrase.

[2] It is extremely difficult to distinguish between the original tradition and the evangelist's additions. Clearly, the evangelist is responsible for the theological theme of Jesus as the light of the world (vv. 3-5), and probably also for the Christological discussion (9.29 f., 35-40).

nection between sickness and sin (9.2-3a). Granted the common Jewish view that sickness was a punishment for sin,[1] why should a man be *born blind*? The rabbis suggested that such cases were due to pre-natal or parental sin. The narrator rejects such explanations, but as the text stands, offers no alternative. Probably his own explanation has been suppressed by the evangelist to make room for vv. 3b-5.

The raising of Lazarus has been so heavily overlaid by the evangelist's own additions that it is very difficult to be sure what comes from his source. Here is a tentative reconstruction:

> Now a certain man was ill, Lazarus of Bethany, the village of Martha and her sister Mary. So the sisters sent to him, saying 'Sir, he whom you love is ill'. When Jesus heard that he was ill, he stayed two days longer in the place where he was. Then, after this, he said to his disciples, 'Let us go into Judea again'. Thus he spoke and then he said to them 'Our friend Lazarus has fallen asleep, but I go to awaken him out of sleep'.
>
> Now when Jesus came, he found that Lazarus had already been in the tomb four days. Many had come to console the sisters concerning their brother. When Jesus saw the sisters weeping, and those who came with them also weeping, he was deeply moved and troubled; and he said, 'Where have you laid him?' They say unto him, 'Sir, come and see'. Then Jesus, deeply moved again, came to the tomb and said, 'Take away the stone'. Martha said to him, 'Sir, by this time there will be an odour, for he has been dead four days!' Jesus lifted up his eyes to heaven and

[1] A view taken for granted in Mark 2.1-12 (the paralytic) and radically criticized at Luke 13.1-5.

> cried with a loud voice, 'Lazarus, come out!' The dead man came out, his hands and feet bound with bandages, and his face wrapped with a cloth. Jesus said to them, 'Unbind him and let him go'.

There are a number of conventional traits in this story. Jesus delays his visit for two days: as at Cana the wonder-worker chooses his own time for the miracle. Then he announces Lazarus' death. As in Mark's story of the leper, he gives a display of emotion (11.33), thus working himself up for the miracle. Lazarus has already been dead for four days and corruption has set in. This makes the miracle more tremendous. Yet the narrator gives the story a Christian meaning. The climax comes in Jesus' words, 'Unbind him and let him go' (11.44). Lazarus is loosed from the bonds of death. The story proclaims Christ's triumph over the powers that hold man in thrall.

Thus, despite their close contact with popular wonder-stories, the miracles in the Book of Signs are truly 'signs' with a real Christian message. They show forth Jesus' Messianic power which was still being manifested in the continuing life of the Christian church.

The Evangelist's Interpretation

As we have already seen, the evangelist reinterprets the signs by the addition of new material. Sometimes he weaves a dialogue into the body of the story. Sometimes he expands an already existing dialogue. Sometimes he makes the miracle a jumping-off point for a new dialogue or discourse in which Jesus is the central speaker. There was precedent for this treatment in the synoptic tradition. The pronouncement stories had used miracles as carriers for a significant saying of Jesus, while nearly all of the miracle stories have dialogue inserted into the body of the narrative. John has simply carried the same process further.[1]

Unlike the other signs, the evangelist has made little change to the marriage at Cana and the official's son. He achieves his reinterpretation mainly by the place in which he inserts them and by the relation they thus acquire to the gospel story as a whole.

By placing the marriage at Cana right at the beginning of the ministry, the evangelist makes it serve a purpose similar to the sermon at Nazareth in Luke. At Cana, Jesus is laying all his cards on the table, and saying in effect, 'Here is the meaning of my whole ministry: it is changing water into wine'. As a result, the traditional features of the story are given a new meaning. Note the phrase, 'My hour has not yet come' (2.4). In the Book of Signs this was a typical trait: the wonder-worker refused to submit to pressure, reserving his own right to decide when to use his miraculous power. For the evangelist, however, this phrase enunciates a theme which runs all through[2] the gospel.

The 'hour' is the hour of the passion. At the marriage at Cana *that* hour has certainly not yet come. Jesus takes his mother's request as a demand to perform the ultimate saving work for which he was sent. The time for this has not yet come, but instead Jesus consents to perform a preliminary sign which will disclose the meaning of his whole ministry and passion. The second

[1] It is assumed that the discourse material is the evangelist's own composition. This does not, however, exclude the probability that it contains traditional sayings of Jesus. Some of these sayings are paralleled in the synoptic tradition, while others have a definite synoptic flavour.

[2] See 4.23; 7.30; 8.20; 12.23, 27; 13.1; 16.32 and 17.1.

trait is the statement[1] that the water in the six jars was 'for the Jewish rites of purification'. The change of this water into wine thus symbolizes the replacement of the purifications of the old dispensation by the Messianic purification: 'The blood of Jesus cleanses us from our sins' (I John 1.7).[2] The third trait is the conclusion, 'Jesus . . . manifested his glory'. In the Book of Signs this probably meant that the miracle was a display of the wonder-worker's power. But, for the evangelist, 'glory' is another key word. It means the revelation of God's presence in saving action, which again reaches its culmination in the passion (13.31; 17.1). The wine which Jesus gives is a symbol of the Messianic salvation, revealed throughout the ministry and supremely accomplished on the cross. It has often been maintained that the Christ of the fourth gospel is a revealer rather than a redeemer. But, as the marriage of Cana shows, the revelation *is* the redemptive act, the Messianic purification.

The evangelist has inserted a generalized summary of miracles at Jerusalem (2.23-25), the purpose of which is to supply Nicodemus with his opening gambit, 'No one can do these signs which you do, unless God is with him'. But it also opens up a theme which is of obvious concern to this gospel writer, namely, the inadequacy of a faith based merely on miracle. Although many believed on him, Jesus would not trust himself to them (v. 24). Genuine faith ought not to rely on miracles (cf. 4.48; 20.29). Not that miracle faith is necessarily bad,

[1] This may have been added by the evangelist, since he is fond of such explanatory remarks, also of allusions to the 'Jews'.

[2] The Greek word for 'cleanses' cames from the same root as 'purification' in John 2.6.

for it *can* lead to true faith, as in the case of Nicodemus, the official (see below), and Thomas (20.28); and in 14.11 the Johannine Christ can say: 'Believe me, that I am in the Father and the Father in me, or else believe me for the *sake of the works themselves*.' To believe in Jesus because of his miracles may be better than nothing, but it is only a second best, a beginning which may lead to genuine faith. Perhaps the evangelist's insistence on the inadequacy of miracle-faith is an attempt to correct the viewpoint of the Book of Signs, or at least a misunderstanding which it might encourage.

In the story of the official's son the evangelist has added only a few touches. The typical cross-reference to the marriage at Cana is due to him (4.46) and so is 4.48, another protest against mere miracle-faith. Inserted here, it strikes the reader as a little harsh. What had the official done to deserve a rebuke? After all, he had only asked for help! The evangelist only wants to make a doctrinal point: Jesus is not a purveyor of mere physical healing. He is the true revelation and saving act of God. Nor are miracles proofs of his authority and status. The official takes no notice of the rebuke (it is really intended for the reader) and repeats his request for help: 'Come down before my child dies.' Seeing that he is genuinely in need, Jesus promises that his son will get better, and the official believes his word. This is more than mere miracle faith. The official is sincerely and energetically grasping for help. But, unlike the synoptists, John is critical even of this kind of faith. It is all right as far as it goes, but it would still be a faith which looks only for physical healing. In v. 53, however, the official and all his household 'believe'. Here, at last, is true faith as the evangelist understands it: acceptance of the Christian proclamation of Jesus as the Revealer and Redeemer.

In the healing of the lame man at Bethesda the evangelist (cf. above p. 93) has added 5.17, 18b. This introduces the theme of the relationship between Jesus and the Father, to be developed in the discourse which he appends in 5.19-47.

In the synoptic tradition Jesus has claimed the right to heal on the sabbath because he was 'doing good'. This, we suggested, was not just a humanitarian act, but the saving work of the Messiah. The Messianic significance of the sabbath healings is brought out more clearly in this discourse: 'My Father is working still and I work' (5.17). The argument is based on a rabbinic speculation. God, we are told, rested from his work on the seventh day (Gen. 2.2). Does this, asked the Rabbis, mean that God is completely idle on the sabbath? No, they answered. He does rest, it is true, from his creative work, but he still passes judgement on sin. This is what Jesus was doing in healing the lame man. For this was a work of judgement as well as salvation; it challenged men to faith or unbelief. Thus Jesus was doing God's work on the sabbath, and this, as the Jews protest, is making himself equal with God (5.18). They are quite right. Jesus is performing on earth God's work of judgement. His authority to do this work of judgement on earth—which is also the work of the Father in heaven—depends on his eternal relationship with the Father (note the present tenses in 5.19, 20) and his obedience within that eternal relationship. Jesus' authority as disclosed in his words and deeds does not rest upon a purely ethical, human obedience to the will of God, nor is it merely the authority of a prophet which rests on his commissioning. It involves his person as well as his work, and is rooted in his eternal relationship with the Father. This, of course, presupposes the pre-existence of the Son, which the evangelist has stated quite clearly in the Prologue (1.1-14).

Now all this seems a far cry from the interpretation of the miracles in the synoptic gospels. But this is not really so. It is saying in different language what Jesus himself meant when he said that he cast out evil spirits by the finger of God, and when he declared that men's reaction to his message would be ratified by the Son of man at the last judgement (Luke 12.8). The Christology which the fourth gospel distils from the miracles of Jesus is couched in a very different idiom from Jesus' self-understanding, yet it is a true interpretation of the historical Jesus. In him we are confronted with the immediate presence and activity of God himself. All this was implicit in Jesus' own understanding of his words and works. It is explicit, though somewhat crudely expressed, in the oral tradition behind the synoptists. But it is formulated most satisfactorily in the words which the fourth evangelist puts into the mouth of Jesus: 'The Son can do nothing by his own accord, but only what he sees the Father doing.' The words and works of the Son are the words and works of the Father because of the eternal relation between the Father and the Son. Finally, the miracles point to the greater works which Jesus will do—in the preaching of the church after the resurrection (5.21-27) and in the final judgement at the last day (vv. 28 f.).

A few touches in the feeding of the multitude may come from the evangelist. In 6.4 he explains that the passover was a 'feast of the Jews', thus preparing the way for the eucharistic teaching in the ensuing discourse (6.26-59). For this addition to v. 14 see above, p. 93 n.

John has apparently left the walking on the water untouched, but keeps it in so as to bring Jesus and the crowd together again, after they had become separated at the discourse in the synagogue at Capernaum. The evangelist does not develop the theological significance of the walking on the water.

The discourse on the eucharist, which interprets the feeding of the multitude, is introduced by a dialogue exposing the right and wrong attitude to miracles (compare 2.23-4; 4.48). 'Truly, truly, I say unto you, you seek me, not because you saw signs, but because you ate your fill of the loaves' (6.26). The Jews did not appreciate the signs as signs in the true, Johannine sense, as pointers away from themselves and symbols of the whole work of God in Christ. They saw in them only miraculous physical satisfaction, to be enjoyed for its own sake. The discourse which follows expounds the feeding as a sign in the Johannine sense. First, the bread which the multitude has received is a sign of the 'bread that remains to eternal life' (v. 27), that 'gives life to the world' (v. 33). Jesus' provision of the bread in the wilderness has reminded them of Moses' provision of the manna. But it is a greater gift than the manna. Jesus is not merely repeating what Moses did (v. 32). The feeding of the multitude is a sign that through Jesus God will give the reality of which the manna was a type, the 'true bread from heaven'. This is John's term for the Messianic banquet. In the life of the church, the word and sacrament are an anticipation of that very banquet, which will be consummated at the resurrection in the last day (vv. 39, 40, 44). But the bread of the Messianic banquet is not a gift detached from the giver. *It is himself: 'I am* the bread of life' (v. 35). The revelation of God which Jesus brings is not a system of theological notions or teachings, but himself, as a person and event, his whole coming into the world and his doing the will of the Father who sent him (v. 38).

To the Jews this is a scandal. How can this man say that he himself is the bread that comes down from heaven? After all they knew where he came from and who his parents were (v. 42). They had him taped! Their objections drive home the paradox. Christian faith finds precisely in Jesus of Nazareth, with all his historical limitations, the very revelation of God. But only faith can understand this; only if God draws a man to Jesus (v. 44), only if the Father gives him to Jesus (v. 37), only if men see the Son and believe in him (v. 40). Faith, like its object, is paradoxical. On the one hand it is the free decision of a man's will, on the other hand the sole gift of God.

In 6.51b the discourse takes a fresh turn. The bread which is Jesus himself is his 'flesh and blood'. The change is so abrupt that some scholars have suspected that vv. 51b-58 are the addition of a later hand. This drastic conclusion, for which there is not a shred of manuscript evidence, misses the point. In the eucharist, what was originally given in the incarnation is made available to men only as a result of the cross. Jesus not only came down into the world to bring life eternal; he makes that life eternal available through, and only through, the cross, only because he lays down his life for the world, and thereby gives his 'flesh and blood' (life that has passed through death) for the life of the world. The two parts of the discourse form an organic whole. The feeding of the five thousand, in the evangelist's interpretation, becomes a symbol of all that the eucharist means in the life of the church: it is the fulfilment of the manna, the anticipation of the Messianic banquet and a participation in Christ's sacrificial death.

To the man born blind the evangelist has added a preface (9.3b-5) which interprets the man's illness as an occasion for the works of God to be made manifest in him. In other words, this miracle, like the others (especially 2.11; 11.4), is to be a symbol of the redemptive work of Jesus as the Light of the world (cf. 1.4; 8.12; 12.35). In the trial scenes (9.13-41) the evangelist has added a few explanatory touches and underlined the Christological theme in the recurring discussion of 'where Jesus comes from' (9.16, 29, 30, 33). The effect is to bring out the contrast between the unbelieving Jews and the man who had been blind. The Jews are secure in their possession of the Mosaic tradition, and therefore blind to the new revelation in Christ. By contrast the blind man had no false sense of security: he knew he was blind, and was therefore open to the revelation of God in Jesus. When the Jews excommunicate him they are showing up their own blindness. So the story, as written by the evangelist, culminates in the declaration:

> For judgement I came into this world,
> that those who do not see may see,
> and that those who see may become blind (9.39).

The work of God, which Jesus performs as the Light of the world, is the work of revelation and judgement. Of this work the healing of the man born blind is a symbol.

In the raising of Lazarus the evangelist has not followed his more usual practice of interpreting the miracle in dialogue or discourse, but instead has inserted his additions into the development of the narrative (11.4, 7-10, 16, 20-27, 40, 41b-42). Verse 4 serves as a title for the miracle (cf. 9.5). It is to be a revelation of the 'glory' of God, a key word we found in the marriage at Cana. Since the cross is the supreme manifestation of the 'glory' or saving action of God in Jesus, the Lazarus miracle serves as a curtain raiser to the passion.

The second insertion, 11.7-10, contains a number of features which are characteristic of the evangelist: first, the reference to 'the Jews', then the typical contrast between light and darkness (cf. 1.5, etc.), and the expression 'walking in darkness' (cf. 12.35; I John 2.10). The point of these embellishments comes out in v. 9: 'Are there not twelve hours in the day?' The time for the signs is limited to Jesus' ministry, which is soon coming to an end in the event to which the signs point, the passion itself.

In the third insertion (11.16) Thomas wants to go and die with Jesus. The purpose of this remark is to keep before the reader the ultimate goal of Jesus' ministry, namely the passion.

These are but minor touches. The miracle's real meaning comes out in the dialogue between Jesus and the sisters (11. 20-32, 40-42). The conversation with Martha traces the successive stages in the growth of her faith. At first she wishes Jesus had arrived sooner. As a good wonder-worker he could then have healed Lazarus before he died. Next, she advances a step further; even now, God can grant whatever Jesus asks for. Jesus then promises her that her brother will rise again. Martha misunderstands him—a typical Johannine device leading up to the great revelation. She thought he meant the resurrection in the last day, which all Jews —except the Sadducees—believed in. Now, at last, comes the climax: 'I am the resurrection and the life' (v. 25). Jesus does not merely preach the Jewish hope of resurrection at the last day. To those who accept him resurrection and life are already available here and now. Through the advent of Jesus into the world the final transition from 'death' to 'life', becomes a present possibility, and therefore, in the evangelist's perspective, a possibility in the preaching and sacraments of the church.

The physical raising of Lazarus follows as a symbol of this transition from death to life already within earthly existence. For all its crudity, it is not superfluous, even after the tremendous declaration of v. 25. It drives home the all-important truth that newness of life in Christ is not just an intellectual notion, but a real event which is consequent upon Jesus' word. It is something that *happens*, not just something talked about, not even something talked about by Jesus. It is an event, consequent upon his person and his work: he *is* the resurrection and the life. Henceforth, for those who have accepted Jesus' word, death, though still a biological occurrence ('though he die'), becomes theologically irrelevant ('yet shall he live'). Martha receives the revelation, and makes a Christian confession of faith (v. 27).

The physical raising of Lazarus is delayed by a second talk with Mary. This serves as a foil to the scene with Martha. Mary begins with the same opening gambit as Martha, but never gets any further. So Jesus gives her no revelation as he did to Martha in v. 25, nor does Mary make any confession of faith. In the last resort she is really no better than the 'Jews'. The emotional displays (33a, 35), originally the typical reactions of a wonder-worker, now acquire a new meaning: they express Jesus' sorrow at the Jews' (and Mary's) lack of faith in him as the resurrection and the life.

In v. 40 the evangelist inserts a reference back to the revelation of v. 25. Martha had then perceived the truth of the revelation, but she was still not yet ready to accept the physical raising of Lazarus as a sign of it. Thus the evangelist again reminds us of the real meaning of the miracle: it is a symbol of the 'glory' of God, his saving action in Christ's death and resurrection.

The final insertion is the prayer of Jesus (vv. 41b-42). To the modern reader this prayer is irritating, if not offensive. The whole thing looks like a put-up show, anything but genuine prayer. Jesus knows he need not pray, but apparently stages a prayer to impress the bystanders! But the real point of it is this. Jesus lives in constant prayer and communication with his Father. When he engages in vocal prayer, he is not entering, as we do, from a state of non-praying into prayer. He is only giving overt expression to what is the ground and base of his life all along. He emerges from non-vocal to vocal prayer here in order to show that the power he needs for his ministry—and here specifically for the raising of Lazarus—depends on the gift of God. It is through that prayer and communion and constant obedience to his Father's will that he is the channel of the Father's saving action. That is why the prayer is a thankgiving rather than a petition—though the Jews, who overhear him praying, would interpret it as a petition. Here we have the most profound aspect of

John's treatment of the miracles. It places Jesus poles apart from the mere wonder-workers, and seeks to penetrate into the mystery of how he, though to all outward appearance an ordinary (or perhaps extraordinary) human being, is the one in whom is disclosed God's presence and his very self in saving action. This passage should be read in conjunction with 5.19 f. and 14.9-11, where John again touches on the mystery of the Son's eternal union with the Father manifested in the 'works'.

This is the last of the Johannine signs. From the Book of Signs the evangelist has taken the final summary (12.37-43) and used it to conclude his own presentation of Jesus' ministry, signs and discourses as well. The whole of the ministry is thus defined as a series of 'signs'. For the whole of the ministry, not the miracles only but also the discourses, had but one meaning: it interprets the revealing, saving action of God in the incarnation, death and resurrection of the Son. The evangelist has seen what was implicit behind the oral tradition of the synoptists, namely that every unit of material, the miracles included, preaches in a nutshell the total redemptive act of God in Christ.

The second half of John's gospel covers the farewell discourses and the passion narrative. Henceforth there are no more miracles. But in the farewell discourses there are allusions to the 'works' (see 14.10 f.; 14.12; 15.24). In 14.12 Jesus speaks of the 'works' which the disciples will do afterwards, *because* he will go to the Father. These works of the disciples are the preaching of the word and the ministry of the sacraments. They are 'greater' than Jesus' miracles, because the latter only symbolized in advance the messianic salvation, whereas the word and sacraments mediate it after its accomplishment.[1] 15.24 looks back to the miracles of Jesus as the confrontation of the Jews with the revelation of God in Christ; to reject this revelation is the ultimate sin.

After the last supper, all further reference to the signs is dropped. For now occurs the supreme event to which the signs had pointed, and to which they had given meaning—the passion and glorification of the Son.

[1] See my *What is Liturgical Preaching?* London, 1957, p. 43.

6

PREACHING THE MIRACLES TODAY

THE ACADEMIC study of the New Testament can be an interesting intellectual exercise, like digging up fossils or examining lepidoptera. But unless it is conducted as a service to the church in its mission to the world, it is a mere pastime. What effect does all this study have on the preaching of the miracles? We assume, of course, that the preacher *will* preach on the miracles. Since miracle stories form the liturgical gospels on nineteen Sundays of the church's year in the Book of Common Prayer (eighteen Sundays in the American Prayer Book), the Anglican preacher has at least a moral duty to preach on them. And even in churches which have no fixed lectionary the miracles form such a striking and characteristic part of the gospel story that the preacher can hardly avoid them.

One thing at least is clear. The preacher cannot today follow Archdeacon Paley and treat the miracles as proofs of Jesus' divinity—not even during the Epiphany season, when he might be tempted to do so. We believe and confess the deity (a better word than divinity) of Jesus Christ, not as a metaphysical abstraction but because the Christian community has throughout the ages experienced in Jesus Christ, in his word and in his sacraments, the redemptive action of God himself: God was—and is—in Christ, reconciling the world to himself. But we do not, and cannot, 'prove' that God is in him. This is truth-in-encounter.

Nor can we treat the miracles as humanitarian examples. There is a place for humanitarian acts in the Christian life. Their motive, however, is not an external imitation of Christ, but the response of love to the love of God in Christ (see the exhortations in the Pauline Epistles). And such love is never merely humanitarian: it is a reflection of that ultimate love of God which deals with the ultimate need of man (his need of redemption) of which sickness is but a parable. When we are expounding passages like the ethical exhortations in the Pauline epistles there will be a place for exhortation to the humanitarian care of the sick. But in preaching on the miracles of Christ—since the evangelists never use the miracles in this way, and since all preaching must be based on what the text says—there is no place for humanitarian exhortation.

What of the church's healing ministry, of which we hear so much today? We can rule out in advance modern secular or quasi-secular 'faith-healing', since the gospel miracles know nothing of this. Nor is there any warrant for treating bodily illness as essentially unreal, in Christian Science fashion. Yet the missionary charges to the apostles in the gospels include the command, 'Heal the sick' (Matt. 10.8), a command which is still given to the Anglican bishop as part of his apostolic ministry.[1] Are the miracles of Jesus relevant to this ministry, and should they be used to promote it? Matthew's treatment of the miracles in Chapters 8-9,

[1] In the exhortation beginning 'Give heed unto reading' at the delivery of the Bible.

followed by the charge to the apostles in Chapter 10, allows, and even demands, that they should be. But these same chapters contain pertinent warnings for the contemporary revival of the church's healing ministry. It must not become the monopoly of cranks. The whole thing must be kept in focus. In the apostolic charges, as in Jesus' own ministry, the healing of the sick is always subordinated to the proclamation of the message (see Matt. 9.35; 10.7 f.). The healings, whether performed by Christ, his apostles, or the contemporary church, are a parable and part of the final redemption of the whole man, body as well as soul. The church can never command, but she must always expect that the power of miraculous healing (in the strict sense of an act of God) may at any time occur in her midst—when and where God chooses. Nor can we deny the place of healing as a special gift of grace in the church, if and when it occurs (I Cor. 12.9 f.), though this aspect of the church's healing ministry would not appear to demand consideration in preaching the miracles of the gospels but only in connection with the epistles. The Pauline qualifications and warnings about the spiritual gifts generally would need to be emphasized here.

How far should the preacher discuss the historicity of the miracles? Hoskyns once said: 'The question we are meant to ask is not, Did they happen? (that is comparatively irrelevant), but, What did they mean to our Lord? and therefore, What do they mean to us?'[1] As we saw in Chapter 2, it is possible and even relevant, in so far as it helps to demonstrate the continuity between Jesus' understanding of the miracles and their interpretation in the post-resurrection church, to

[1] *Cambridge Sermons*, pp. 58 f.

establish the *general* historicity of the healing miracles and the exorcisms. After all, it is no good speaking of the meaning of our Lord's miracles if he never did any! To this extent it is relevant to establish their general historicity, and pastoral necessity demands that the preacher should frankly face up to the question, if only to demonstrate its 'comparative irrelevance'. The preacher's chief concern, however, must be the meaning of the miracles for us, for his hearers today. He must first establish the meaning of the miracles in the text before him, and then relate that meaning to the contemporary situation. Since modern historical investigation of the gospel material has provided him with the necessary tools, he can start from the biblical meaning of the miracles at several different levels: their meaning to Jesus, to the oral tradition (the narrators), and to the evangelists. At each stage, we saw, the narrators and the evangelists never created new meanings, but unfolded meanings which were already latent in the tradition. The preacher's task is to carry this process a stage further.

A careful examination of their procedure shows that the narrators and the evangelists were interested in the miracles not as past events, but as illustrations of what the risen Christ was doing in his church in their own day. They were not interested in the sick people who came to or who were brought to the Lord for their own sake, as historical persons, but as types of the men and women who heard the gospel in the church. The plight of the sick folk in Galilee was the plight of those who came to the living Lord. The healing word and act of the Saviour were the word which he spoke and the act which he performed in the word and sacraments. Despite the sentimentality of the third line, the Victorian hymn has caught the basic conviction behind the miracle stories:

> Thy touch has still its ancient power;
> No word from thee can fruitless fall;
> Hear, in this solemn evening hour,
> And in thy mercy heal us all.

Taking his cue, then, from the narrators and evangelists, the preacher will seek to show that the predicament of the paralytic, the blind, the deaf, and the dead who came to (or were brought to) Jesus in Galilee is the predicament of modern man. The contemporary preacher must make Jesus' word of healing a living address to his hearers, and exhibit the touch of Jesus in the sacraments. The gospel miracles are not tales of what happened in far-off Palestine two thousand years ago, but proclamations of the works of Christ today.

We now propose to give four examples of the way the miracles of the gospels might be treated in contemporary preaching. The four examples are taken from the liturgical gospels of the Book of Common Prayer, one from each of the main seasons, Advent, Epiphany, Lent and Trinity-tide. The warning given elsewhere[1] must be borne in mind here: 'These examples must not be regarded as skeleton sermons, nor even as suggestions of what should actually be said in the pulpit. They are merely indications of the preliminary theological spadework which has to be done before a sermon can be constructed.'

The Answer to John (Matt. 11.2-10)[2]

This is not a miracle story, but it contains our Lord's

[1] *What is Liturgical Preaching?* p. 26.
[2] The gospel for Advent III.

own interpretation of his miracles. We are not meant to ask the historical question, How can John the Baptist have asked this when he was present at the baptism of Jesus? John comes in here only because he asks 'Art thou he that should come?' John is the mouthpiece of the Jewish Messianic hope:

They all were looking for a king.

They were all looking for God's final intervention, when he would put an end to all injustice and unrighteousness and suffering on earth, and establish his kingdom of righteousness and peace. The Messianic hope was the quest of those who would not and could not believe that 'God's in his heaven, all's right with the world'. It is out of this hope that the Baptist's question springs: 'Art thou he that should come?' This should be our question too. Not only because it is Advent, but because the Advent situation is the situation of the world in which we live, a world which knows that all is not right with itself, a world which (though it would not put it like that) is 'looking for a king'. Amid the conflicting voices that offer a 'king' to the modern world—Marxism, scientific humanism and the rest—the Christian church points to Jesus as the king who came and still comes, as the one who has changed the world. And after 2,000 years of Christian history the world asks, in scornful irony or anxious hope: 'Art *thou* he that should come, or do we look for another?'

As so often, Jesus does not answer the question directly, but points to his miracles and to his preaching, challenging John to make up his own mind: 'Blessed is he, whosoever shall not be offended in me.' The miracles are not proofs: to Jesus' enemies they were black magic.

But they are pointers, signs which call for a decision. And the most important sign is, 'the poor have the gospel preached to them'. The miracles are part of the good news, the beginning of God's redemptive action which the preaching heralds.

To what miracles can the church point today? Let the preacher beware of blowing the church's own trumpet by pointing to the achievements of the Christian church in the history of civilization! To the world these are neither miracles nor proofs. The world can always point to the other side of the picture: 'So potent was Religion in persuading to evil deeds' (Lucretius). The church can only point to the works of the Christ in her midst, the preaching of the word and the ministry of the sacraments. To those who have really experienced them, the hope of the world has been realized: 'If any one is in Christ, he is a new creation; the old has passed away, behold, the new has come.' 'Art thou he that should come?' The question can only be answered by those who are prepared to see and hear the works of Christ in his church today—the word and sacraments. We are challenged to see in them, ever anew, the advent of him that should come:

New advent of the love of Christ,
   Shall we again refuse thee?
Till in the night of hate and war
   We perish as we lose thee?
From old unfaith our souls release
To seek the kingdom of thy peace
   By which alone we choose thee.[1]

[1] Walter Russell Bowie: *The Hymnal*, 1940, No. 522.

The Marriage at Cana (St John 2.1-11)[1]

The guests at the wedding and the governor of the feast, who was responsible for seeing that everything was in order, were at the end of their resources: 'They have no wine.' Humanly speaking, there was nothing they could do about it. True, they had something—'six water-pots of stone, after the manner of the purifying of the Jews'—but not the wine that was needed. The wedding, then, is first of all, a parable of the Jews' situation. To man in his predicament Judaism offered a religion. But: 'According to this arrangement gifts and sacrifices are offered (the Jews' purifications!), which cannot perfect the conscience of the worshipper' (Heb. 9.9). 'It is impossible that the blood of bulls and goats should take away sins' (Heb. 10.4). All possibilities within this world, even human religions and philosophies, are powerless to rescue man from his ultimate predicament. For all human piety and all human intellectual activity are still the activities of fallen man. But, at the very point where the marriage party is out of supplies, Jesus takes command of the situation: 'Fill the water pots with water. . . . Draw out now, and bear unto the governor of the feast.' There is wine enough for the guests, and more. The Messianic purification replaces the Jewish purifications: 'how much more shall the blood of Christ, who through the eternal spirit offered himself without blemish to God, purify your conscience from dead works to serve the living God?' (Heb. 9.14). 'The blood of Jesus his Son cleanses us from all sin' (I John 1.7). Here is the epiphany: in the marriage at Cana, a preliminary epiphany ('manifested

[1] The gospel for Epiphany II (American BCP: Epiphany III).

forth his glory'); in the 'hour' of the cross, the supreme epiphany; in the word and sacraments, the extension of that epiphany here and now. Here, where we are at the end of our resources, where we have no wine, where we cannot rescue ourselves from our predicament, Jesus manifests his glory (i.e. the saving presence and action of God) and proves himself master of the situation.

> . . . at Cana, wedding guest,
> In thy Godhead manifest;
> Manifest in power divine,
> Changing water into wine;
> Anthems be to thee addrest,
> God in man made manifest.[1]

The changing of water into wine is not something that happened long ago: it is something that happens in our midst, as we become new creatures in Christ. But it happens because of what Christ did at Cana and on Calvary.

The Dumb Demon (St Luke 11.14-28)[2]

The exorcism is not important in itself, but for the sayings which follow. Indeed, it was probably created as a carrier for the sayings, though of course the sayings themselves presuppose that Jesus did perform exorcisms. The critical remark of Jesus' opponents, 'He casteth out devils through Beelzebul the chief of the devils' is a misinterpretation of the exorcisms which calls forth from Jesus the true interpretation. They are signs of the coming of the Messianic age, the Reign of God. God's Reign is being established by the overthrow

[1] From the hymn by Christopher Wordsworth.
[2] The gospel for Lent III.

of the Reign of Satan. This is what is actually happening in the exorcisms. The point is illustrated by two brief parables: the divided kingdom and house, and the strong man. Appended to this are a number of sayings loosely connected with the theme of exorcism. Neutrality in the warfare between Christ and Satan is impossible (v. 23). A warning is given against letting the evil spirits return after an exorcism (vv. 24-26). Finally there is the crushing reply to the flattery of a silly woman: 'Blessed are they that hear the word of God and keep it' (v. 28).

A strange miscellany of sayings! Yet the early church had an 'existential' reason for selecting this passage as the gospel for the third Sunday in Lent. For it was now that the 'scrutinies' of the catechumens began, in preparation for their baptism, which was to take place on Easter Even. They too must realize that they are now passing over from the kingdom of Satan to the kingdom of God. They too must be warned of the danger of neutrality in the conflict with evil and the dangers of a relapse. They too must be warned of the danger of enjoying religion for its own sake, and must be reminded that the purpose of it all is to hear the word of God and keep it.

Our modern observance of Lent will be put on a sounder theological basis if it is regarded not as an occasion for stepping up acts of individual piety, but as the time when the whole Christian community returns, as it were, to the catechumenate, and prepares for the renewal of its baptism at Easter. This will give an existential relevance to our communal liturgical experience of the Lenten season. We too are now being exorcized, and we too are warned of the dangers that face us. Of course, we no longer believe in demons: 'It is impossible to use electric light and the wireless and to avail ourselves of modern medical and surgical discoveries, and at the same time to believe in the New Testament world of spirits and miracles' (R. Bultmann). But we are bound to believe in what the demons of the New Testament signify. We need not *eliminate* the devil from the catechism but we must *interpret* what he stands for. He stands for the supra-personal reality of evil, something outside ourselves which gets us in its grip. The old mythology may still be used, but it must be understood as a symbolic expression of the realities of human experience. So then, in our baptism the power of evil has been exorcized from our lives. But this is not something that happened once for all as an assured possession; it is something that has to be constantly renewed. We are committed to be Christ's soldiers and servants unto our life's end, manfully fighting under his banner against sin, the world and the devil. In this warfare there is no neutrality. We must be constantly on our guard lest the powers of evil return, and our last state becomes worse than the first: 'It is impossible to restore again to repentance those who have once been enlightened . . . if they then commit apostasy' (Heb. 6.4-6). Christian discipleship is a serious business: there is no place for mere aesthetic enjoyment of religion. We must hear the word of God, as we are hearing it in our Lenten instructions as catechumens, all over again, and keep it.

The Miraculous Draft of Fishes (St Luke 5.1-11)[1]

This is one of the rare instances of a nature miracle

[1] The gospel for Trinity V.

among the liturgical gospels in the Book of Common Prayer.[1] Since it is the nature miracles which raise for modern man the question of the authenticity of the gospel miracles in its acutest form, this is the time to deal with this problem, if only with Hoskyns to demonstrate its 'comparative irrelevance'. Modern man necessarily works with the assumption that normally (even if scientists have been compelled to postulate an element of indeterminacy on the microcosmic scale) there are no miracles, in the sense of breaches of the natural order. What may seem unaccounted for under our present knowledge of nature will, we believe, become explicable with the advance of science. Coming to the New Testament miracles, modern man is prepared to accept the healings of Jesus as due to his power of suggestion: the nature miracles, such as that in today's gospel, he can only dismiss as pious legend.

Here the fundamentalist objects that belief in *all* the biblical miracles is a necessary part of the Christian faith. He demands a sacrifice of the intellect. Doctors and scientists who are fundamentalist Christians—and there are many of them—have made precisely this sacrifice, with the result that their professional and religious lives have become completely departmentalized.

There are two objections to the fundamentalist position. First, it results in intellectual insincerity. It is the Christian's responsibility to follow the truth wherever it leads him. Second, it misunderstands what faith really is. Faith is not believing that such things as the miraculous draft of fishes really happened. It is believing

[1] The English BCP (not American) has the stilling of the storm on Epiphany IV.

in Jesus Christ as my Saviour, as the one in whom God has acted finally for my salvation. To such a faith, the historicity of this or that miracle in the gospel tradition is 'comparatively irrelevant'.

But the fundamentalists have a point. We cannot eliminate the nature miracles from the gospel. The modern Christian who finds relevance for preaching only in those miracles whose historicity he can accept is eliminating an essential part of the apostolic witness. And by denying the truly miraculous nature of those which he does accept, he is evacuating them of their evangelical content. For the miracles, nature or healing, proclaim to us a God of miracles, a God who acts, who intervenes and interferes in specific events. Therefore, what the fundamentalists are really trying to do is to get us to hear the apostolic, evangelic witness behind these stories.

Could we come to a gentleman's agreement about this question, which so divides Christians today?[1] Could we agree to live and let live, and say to the fundamentalist, 'All right, you continue taking for granted the historicity of the miraculous draft of fishes. Intellectual integrity compels me to doubt it. But for both of us that is really neither here nor there.' Whether we take its historicity for granted (as the evangelist did) or not, the real point lies, *as it did for the evangelist*, elsewhere. It is over that real point that the fundamentalist and the modern critical believer can agree. For the evangelist, the real miracle was not the draught of the fishes, but

[1] There is a credal as well as a biblical fundamentalism. Witness the recent outcry in the American churches about Bishop Pike's utterances on the Virgin Birth and in England the correspondence in the *Church Times* (1961) which followed Professor Lampe's article in that journal on the 'Historic Christ'.

the call of Peter to the apostleship and his apostolic ministry. This interpretation is not a modern subterfuge, a *solution d'embarrassment* for a sceptic whose faith has been corroded by the acids of modernity. It represents the true intention of the evangelist.

Peter has toiled all that night and has taken nothing. But at the very point where he is at the end of his tether, the miraculous intervention occurs: 'Launch out into the deep.' In the face of utter absurdity, Peter obeys: 'Nevertheless, *at thy word*. . . .' Peter succeeds where previously he had failed. But in the moment of success, he confesses that it was not he, but Christ who did it. He is only a sinner: 'Depart from me, for I am a sinful man, O Lord.' He has been privileged to be only a channel of that miracle. Then the symbolic meaning of the miracle is made clear: 'Fear not: from henceforth thou shalt catch men.' Here is the point of the tale. It was not really about a miraculous catch of fishes. It was about the call of Peter to be an apostle. Precisely where a man knows that human resources are incapable of solving the ultimate riddle of human life, that no ideology and no political programme can save, there Christ steps in and calls that man to be his apostle. When such a man rises and acts in obedience to Christ's call in face of its utter absurdity, then he is privileged to become the agent and channel of the miracles of God. He can catch men. He? No, the living Christ who uses him. All he can say is: 'Depart from me, for I am a sinful man, O Lord.'

This was the real intention of St Luke in narrating this story. He took its historicity for granted, but that is neither here nor there. It was the call of Peter to be a fisher of man that mattered.

Appendix

THE SPIRITUAL INTERPRETATION OF THE MIRACLES

IN HIS recent book, *The Significance of the Synoptic Miracles* (London, 1961, pp. 77-102), James Kallas makes a vigorous protest against the spiritual or symbolic interpretation of the miracles. He is particularly critical of Alan Richardson's treatment of the feeding of the multitude (*The Miracle Stories of the Gospels*, London, 1st ed., 1941), but he also opposes the spiritual interpretation of the miracles generally.

On the feeding, Kallas asks, 'How do the synoptic accounts of the event entitle Richardson to refer to them and the bread as "spiritual food?" Where does it imply that it is their souls being nourished and not their bodies fed?' Of course, it is true that Mark and the other evangelists (including the Fourth Gospel) take it for granted that the feeding actually happened as a physical miracle. But this does not prevent them from giving the physical feeding a symbolic significance. In particular, Schweitzer's interpretation of the feeding as a symbol of the Messianic banquet, which Kallas castigates together with Richardson's interpretation as a 'flight of fancy', has a firm basis in the actual texts (see above, pp. 57 f., 102 f.), which Kallas' own interpretation as a reassertion of God's kingly rule over Satan's rule does not have.

While it is true that in the oral tradition the healings of the blind are actual physical miracles, and while Mark also takes it for granted that they are so, that does not prevent him from giving them a further symbolic or spiritual meaning. This he does by placing the cure of the blind man of Bethsaida just before the opening of the disciples' eyes to Jesus' Messiahship at Caesarea Philippi, and blind Bartimaeus after the opening of their eyes to the necessity of the cross at the transfiguration. And this spiritual or symbolic significance of the blindness is clinched at 8.18.

The basic weakness of Kallas' treatment is his failure to distinguish between the various levels in the synoptic tradition—Jesus, the oral tradition, the primary sources Mark and Q, and the later evangelists, Matthew and Luke. In other words, he neglects source and form criticism, as the key to the exegesis. Consequently he attributes an identical theology to all layers of the tradition, and he assigns them all far too readily to Jesus himself.

LIST OF GOSPEL MIRACLES WITH INDEX

Markan

Mark 1.21-28/Luke 4.36-37: The Capernaum demoniac, 35 and n., 48 f., 54 n., 70, 75, 76 n., 84

Mark 1.39-41/Matt. 8.14-15/Luke 4.38-39: Simon's mother-in-law, 34, 35, 49, 70, 77, 84

Mark 1.32-34/Matt. 8.16-17/Luke 4.40-41: Healings at eventide, 70, 72, 73, 75, 76 n.

Mark 1.40-44/Matt. 8.1-4/Luke 5.12-16: The Leper, 49 f., 71, 75, 77, 78, 81, 84, 85 n.

Mark 2.1-12/Matt. 9.1-8/Luke 5.17-26: The paralytic, 35 and n., 42, 50 ff., 56, 71, 73, 76 n., 77, 84, 85 n., 86, 91, 95 n.

Mark 3.1-6/Matt. 12.9-14/Luke 6.6-11: The withered hand, 52 f., 71, 79, 84

Mark 3.7-12/Matt. 12.15-21/Luke 6.17-19: Galilean healings, 35 n. 72, 73, 75, 76 n., 79

Mark 4.35-41/Matt. 8.23-27/Luke 8.22-25: The stilling of the storm, 38, 53 f., 72, 77, 81

Mark 5.1-20/Matt. 8.28-34/Luke 8.26-39: The Gerasene demoniac (Matt.: The Gadarene demoniacs), 34, 35 and n., 54 f., 72, 73, 77, 81

Mark 5.21-43/Matt. 9.18-26/Luke 8.40-56: The daughter of Jairus and the woman with the haemorrhage, 36 f., 42, 55 ff., 72, 73, 75, 77, 81, 85 n., 90

Mark 6.30-34/Matt. 14.13-21/Luke 9.10-17: The feeding of the 5,000, 37, 57 f., 74, 79 f.

Mark 6.45-52/Matt. 14.22-33: Walking on the water, 38, 58 f., 74, 79 f., 86

Mark 6.53-55/Matt. 14.31-36: Healings in Gennesaret, 35 n., 79

Mark 7.24-30/Matt. 15.21-28: The Syro-Phoenician woman (Matt.: The Canaanitish woman), 42, 48, 59 f., 74, 79 f., 81, 86

Mark 7.31-37: The deaf mute, 34, 55, 60 f., 74, 79 f., 86

Mark 8.1-10/Matt. 15.32-39: The feeding of the 4,000, 37, 60 f., 74, 75, 86, 91

Mark 8.22-26: The blind man of Bethsaida, 34, 60 f., 74, 75, 77, 86, 91

Mark 9.14-29/Matt. 17.14-21/Luke 9.37-43a: The epileptic boy, 34, 35 and n., 61 f., 81, 85 n.

Mark 10.46-53/Matt. 20.29-34/Luke 18.35-43: Blind Bartimaeus, 35, 42, 56, 62 f., 74, 77, 81, 85 n., 86, 91

Mark 11.12-14/Matt. 21.18-22: The cursing of the fig tree, 38 f., 63, 74

Matt. 8.5-13/Luke 7.1-10: The centurion's boy, 37, 42, 48, 77, 81

Matt. 4.23: Healings in the Galilean synagogues, 78
Matt. 9.27-31: The two blind men, 25 n., 77, 81
Matt. 9.32-34: The dumb demoniac, 25 n., 78
Matt. 9.35: Healings in the Galilean cities, 78
Matt. 12.22: The blind and dumb demoniac, 25 n., 32
Matt. 14.14: Healings in the wilderness, 25 n., 89
Matt. 15.29-31: Healings on the mountain, 79
Matt. 19.2: Healings in Transjordan, 25 n.
Matt. 21.14: Healings in the temple, 25 n.

Luke 5.1-11: The miraculous draft of fishes, 37, 63, 84, 120 ff.
Luke 7.11-17: The widow's son at Nain, 36 f., 64, 85 n., 86, 90
Luke 7.21: Healings at the answer to John, 86
Luke 9.11: Healings at Bethsaida, 89
Luke 13.10-17: The bent woman, 64, 83
Luke 14.1-6: The dropsical man, 65, 83
Luke 22.51: The high priest's servant's ear, 25, 83 n.

John 2.1-11: The marriage at Cana, 19, 57, 89, 90 f., 97 f., 104, 117 f.
John 2.23-25: Signs at Jerusalem, 98
John 4.46-54: The official's son, 17, 37 n., 89, 90, 91, 93, 98, 99 f.
John 5.1-18: The lame man at Bethesda, 89, 90, 91, 93 f., 100
John 6.1-13: The feeding of the 5,000, 89, 90, 91, 92, 94, 101
John 6.16-21: The walking on the water, 89, 90, 91, 94, 102
John 9.1-34: The man born blind, 89, 90, 91, 94 f., 104, 105
John 11.1-44: The raising of Lazarus, 49, 89, 90, 91 f., 95 f., 104, 105 ff.

SAYINGS REFERRING TO MIRACLES

Mark 3.30-33/Matt. 12.22-37/Luke 11.14-23 (24-28): The Beelzebul Controversy (also Q), 12, 23, 26 ff., 28 n., 32, 39 ff., 42, 72, 79
Mark. 8.14-21/Matt. 16.5-12: Discourse on the feedings, 74, 76, 78 f., 86, 125
Mark 11.20-25/Matt. 21.20-22: Discourse on the fig tree, 43
Matt. 11.2-6/Luke 7.18-23: The answer to John, 14, 16, 27 f., 41, 47, 56
Matt. 11.20-24/Luke 10.13-15: Woes on the Galilean cities, 28 n., 42
Matt. 13.16-17/Luke 10.23-24: The blessedness of the disciples, 28
Luke 13.32: The message to Herod, 25, 29, 83
John 5.19-47: On the sabbath healing, 100, 108
John 6.26-59: On the bread of life, 102 ff.
John 9.35-40: On the Light of the World, 94, 104

INDEX OF AUTHORS AND SUBJECTS

Apollonius of Tyana, 64
Augustine, 8

Biblical Criticism, 12, 20, 113
Biblical Theology, 14
Bornkamm, G., 14 n., 29 n., 62
Bultmann, R., 26 n., 120

Christian Science, 111
Compassion, 13 f.
Cranfield, C. B. E., 43

Dibelius, M., 26 n.
Dionysus, 19, 90
Discipleship, 81 f.

Epidaurus, 22, 23

Faith, 9, 12, 42 *ff.*, 50, 56, 61 f., 63, 81, 121 f.
Fiebig, P., 21
Form Criticism, 26 f., 30 ff., 55
Fundamentalism, 121 f.

Gardner-Smith, P., 91
Glover, T. R., 12 n.

Hanina, 22
Harnack, A. von, 12 n.
Healing—church's ministry of, 111 f.
Hoskyns, E. C., 13, 14, 61, 65, 66 f., 112, 131

Jeremias, J., 93 n.
Johanan, 21
Josephus, 23

Kallas, J., 12
Kingdom of God, 15, 27, 40 ff., 47, 59, 65, 93, 118
Klausner, J., 23 n.

Lewis, C. S., 8 n.
Liberalism, 12
Lightfoot, R. H., 34 n.
Lucretius, 116

Manson, T. W., 14
Manson, W., 14
McGinley, L. J., 22 n.
Messiahship of Jesus, 14 f., 23, 41 f., 46 ff., 71 f., 78, 94, 98, 100, 115 f., 125
Miracles
as epiphanies, 54, 91, 117 f.
exoricisms, 19, 23, 25 ff., 30 ff., 39 ff., 54, 72, 86, 118 ff.
of healing, 12. 13, 19, 25 ff., 30 ff., 41 ff.
historicity of, 18 ff., 24 ff., 29 ff., 112 ff., 118 ff.
nature, 12, 19, 37 *ff.*, *120 ff.*
number of, 25, 89
Old Testament, 10, 15 f., 57 f., 60 f., 64, 66, 79 f., 83 f., 102
pagan,, 22 55, 64, 92, 94
Pauline, 20 ff.
as proofs, 11 ff., 44 f., 87, 110, 115
psychologically explained, 12, 39
rabbinical, 21 f., 31, 54
raisings, 21, 25, 36 *f.*, 55 ff., 72, 77, 85 n., 86, 89, 90, 91 f., 95 f., 105 ff.
vocabulary of, *15 ff.*

Nowell-Smith, P., 8 n.

Paley, W., 11 f., 110
Prayer, 21, 42, 107

Ramsey, I., 8 n.
Rationalism, 12, 19
Redlich, E. B., 26 n.
Remission of sins, 57 f.
Richardson, A., 14, 91, 92, 124

Taylor, V., 14, 26 n.
Tractate Sanhedrin, 23
Turner, H. E. W., 14, 33, 38